THE
ROAD
NORTH

One Woman's Adventure Driving
the Alaska Highway
1947-1948

Text and Photos by Iris Woolcock

from the Woolcock Collection,
Anchorage Museum of History and Art

edited by Edward Bovy

Greatland Graphics   Anchorage

Editor's Note

Iris Woolcock's original manuscript was more than 120,000
words. Approximately 15,000 words were lost through the
years.

I have condensed some of her travelogue, primarily those
portions of the trip taking place in the continental U. S.
Since the original text was one long narrative, I also
added chapter headings to facilitate reading.

The Woolcock Collection also includes more than 500 photos.
A representative sample is included here. Many other
Woolcock photos were lost as described in her adventure.

Her long time friend, Peggy Isphording, recognized the
value of this work and donated the manuscript to the Anchorage Museum of History and Art in hopes that it would be
of value to someone someday. We are all indebted to her
for her foresightedness in this regard.

E. B.

Library of Congress Catalogue Card Number: 90-82429

THE ROAD NORTH

Dedicated to all who travel the Alaska Highway

A thousand miles from nowhere,
A thousand miles to go
How long how long,
Nobody seems to know.

Norman Rosten
"The Big Road"
1946

Iris Woolcock was born in Wisconsin in the late 1800's and died in 1980.

She was an artist, photographer, realtor and adventuress; for example, she spent a lot of time in Central America photographing the fruit plantations for one of the big companies.

Iris lived in Putney (Vermont), New York City, and in later years in Warm Mineral Springs, Florida. Among her close friends were Buckminster Fuller and Ellsworth Bunker.

Iris was one of those incredibly vibrant people who lived life to its fullest. At age 67 she set a deep dive record at Warm Mineral Springs. She was an accomplished artist and painted a portrait of Liza Minelli's father.

She had so many varied interests, she never quite managed to settle down and really stick with any of them— art, journalism, photography, or her diving. She at one time tried to have her Alaska travels published but was on to other projects long before she passed the text on to me shortly before she died.

Iris was a great believer in good nutrition and preventative medicine. She always wore a glamorous wide-brimmed hat, lots of makeup and drove a bright red Ford convertable until her death.

For all her adventuring, she was a very private person. She had one son but never remarried after a divorce early in life.

Iris was, above all else, a renaissance woman. It's too bad she isn't a young woman in this day and age; she did a lot of the things young ladies are doing now only much earlier in time.

I was so fortunate to be among her friends. I am sure she would be tickled to know that her account of her adventure to Alaska finally was published. Then again maybe she does know as she was a bit of a clairvoyant too.

Peggy Isphording
Venice, Florida

Iris Woolcock

Fairbanks,
Alaska ★

Whitehorse,
★ Yukon Territory

C A N A D A

Dawson Creek,
British Columbia

★ Edmonton, Alberta

Havre,
Montana

★ Putney, Vermont

Breman,
Indiana

★ Washington, D.C.

U N I T E D   S T A T E S

MEXICO

Warm Mineral
Springs, Florida

THE TRAVELS OF IRIS WOOLCOCK

1. BULLS, GATORS AND MIDNIGHT SWIMS

I couldn't sleep. I was really scared. No one will believe me when I say I could smell and feel the hot breath of the huge Brahma bull through the open windows of the little trailer. The bull was snorting and pawing and walking round and round it. In his attempt to brush off flies or mosquitoes he was demolishing the palms which had been planted a few feet from the trailer door. The door was open. Would he attempt to barge in through the screen door even though it was much too narrow? Would he charge the trailer? If he did, he'd crash right through. Thank heavens he didn't know it was nothing but pasteboard.

That was my first night in a trailer. It was parked away off by itself in a sort of no man's land half way between Venice and Punta Gorda in southwestern Florida. There was a marvelous warm salt spring there which was working a miraculous cure on my broken back. Whether it was the chemical content of the water, or the warmth, or the exercise of swimming, I'll never know. But I do know I loved swimming in it for hours every day and wanted some more of it before heading back north to my farm in Vermont.

For a time I had driven down from Sarasota every day but that was a long trip. When I tried an apartment in Venice which was a close to the spring as it was possible to live, I didn't like it. A solitary trailer had been left down at the spring by a dealer in hopes of renting it or selling it. Rental and purchase price had seemed too exorbitant to anyone interested. The winter season was over and there it still sat. One day when I was swimming, the dealer came to take it away. I told him to hold on a minute. "If you'll leave that there and rent it to me a couple of weeks at a very reasonable price you'll be just that much ahead." He agreed and I moved in.

To be able to live right there on the brink of my beloved pool and even add a midnight swim to my schedule, merely changing from one bathing suit to another day after day—that was surely what the doctor ordered.

No one knew how deep that pool was. The water bubbled up from goodness knows where. Some men had tried to plumb the depth but their weight was not heavy enough to go down further than 2,900 feet and they had not been back to try again.

I wasn't afraid of the depth. And I wasn't afraid of the alligators that swam around with me once in awhile. I enjoyed the schools of tarpon I could see below in the clear depths. I didn't mind a few big black snakes —they were harmless.

But I did NOT like that bull. I had been warned to watch out for those Brahma bulls.

This particular bull kept me from having my midnight swim three nights in a row. Finally, on the fourth night, I became exasperated and brave enough to open the door and say, "Shoo!" Off he ran and never came back.

The longer I lived in that little trailer the more I wanted one. To be able to live just anywhere— that is what appealed to me. The anywhere would have to be all it implied as far as I was concerned. I knew I would never consider owning a trailer if I had to depend on trailer parks. And for me it would have to be a mobile photographic laboratory. I couldn't afford to have one unless I could carry my work around with me and make the investment pay.

I began to look at trailers. It was the end of April and all of Florida's winter guests had returned north. Many had left trailers behind to be sold. The market was flooded. They were parked here, there and everywhere with For Sale signs.

The more I looked the more bewildered I became. How was I to judge comparative values and know just which one would be best suited for my purposes? There seemed some awfully good buys. I stopped by Sellhorn Fitzhugh's completely exhausted. I was worried about my lack of knowledge about trailers. I knew that for me it was a tremendous step and big gamble to invest what it would take to get myself equipped with a really good one. And I knew that it had to be very well made and reliable for me to use as I planned to use it a lot— possibly on the road to Alaska.

The place had closed for the evening but Mr. Fitzhugh was standing out in front and when he came to my car to talk to me I said, "I'm tired and bewildered. I want to buy a trailer and I've seen so many I can't make up my mind what I want. I'd like to put my confidence in someone who knows a lot more about them than I do. I'd like to tell you the purpose for which I wish to use the trailer and then rely completely upon your judgment as to which one I should buy."

Fitzhugh's Inc. were big dealers and carried many makes and models of new and used trailers. They were the ones from whom I had been renting the little one down by the spring.

Mr. Fitzhugh said, "Have you had dinner yet?"

"No I haven't" I said, "and I'm not only tired, I'm also very hungry."

"Then won't you dine with me? I'm hungry too and we can talk over this trailer business while enjoying some good food."

I told him then that I wanted to make a trailer serve for a very efficient photographic laboratory both on the road and when at home on my farm in Vermont. I also told him that the type with light tight sliding doors between rooms would be practical for my work, and I said my equipment was heavy. I wanted to be assured of an adequate supply of running water when traveling and parking where I could not hook up to a water system. I wanted two stainless or enamel sinks to facilitate the washing of films and prints, and also a hot water heater.

Mr. Fitzhugh said there was a 27-foot Alma in one of his lots in Tampa which would be ideal for my purpose, a good sturdy tandem with doors dividing into three rooms. The price was pretty high, yet not out of line if it was all he said it was—a trailer of exceptional quality and durability and just like new.

I said again, "I'm leaving it to you. If you say that is the trailer I should have I'll take it."

Late the next afternoon he took me to Tampa in his new Lincoln to see it and bring it down to Sarasota. On the way up he kept telling me what a beautiful trailer it was—just exactly like new, having been occupied only two weeks by a couple who were with Ringling Brothers. Their son came out of the army just after they bought the trailer so they exchanged it for two smaller trailers.

It was getting dark when we reached the lot and I couldn't see the trailer very well. It had a davenport, but it didn't have an electric refrigerator. Fitzhugh said they would put one in.

When we stopped for gas on the way back with it, I checked the tires under the light of the service station. To me they appeared rather ancient and unhealthy. But Mr. Fitzhugh said, "Oh those tires are all right. They'll give you at least a year's good service."

It was exciting to ride along with the huge thing following us. Fitzhugh drove just as though it wasn't there at all, zipping in and out of traffic. "Oh you'll get used to it quickly and forget it's there. Just drive natural and remember it's like a big signboard that everyone else can see. They won't want to hit it. Give yourself a little more room on sharp turns and after you overtake a car or truck don't cut back in too quickly."

Then he told me to come down next day and he'd go over all the details with the men in the shop and give them instructions as to just how I wanted it fixed.

2. A TEST DRIVE

It was a peculiar conference the next morning with the shop foreman trying to argue down everything Fitzhugh suggested. The foreman didn't like trailers anyway, nor did he show any respect for his boss. But Fitzhugh kept insisting that things could be done and finally persuaded him to go to work at it. The men were to put a 50-gallon water tank under the bed and a little electric pump which would work from the tank or from a brook or spring along side of which I might park. Or by turning a few valves I could operate from city pressure. A hot water heater, the two sinks, and a garbage disposal toilet were also to be installed.

It was a simple matter to enlarge one closet to give better storage space and make it possible to shut myself in it in case I found it necessary to change film or open up a camera in the dark. That also made a nice corner in the living room for a row of book shelves.

I wanted to be sure to have good clearance for bad roads so they changed the springs from below to above the axles, adding an extra leaf for strength. And I wanted bumpers because I felt the need for some protection in back.

But whenever I appeared at the shop no one ever seemed to be working on the trailer. They always had some excuse. Time was passing and I became exasperated. Fitzhugh had gone back to his home office in Michigan.

When they told me the springs, wheels, and tires were all in order I took another look at the rubber. One tire looked completely shot. I went into the office and told the manager to go out and see whether he'd start out on a trip with any such tires.

I followed him out and since I was wearing soft-soled sandals, he did not hear me behind him. Neither did the mechanic he questioned. The grouchy mechanic said, "Of course those tires are no good. Can't you see they are antiques that are all worn out? There's one there that won't go a mile."

The fellow who was painting the roof saw and heard it all and gave me a sympathetic smile, but that didn't help matters much. When the manager turned and saw me standing there he said he'd order a set of new tires and let me have them at cost. I told him I was buying a trailer which supposedly had good tires on it and should certainly not be expected to buy a new set before I moved it out of the shop. All I could do was get him to replace the one the mechanic had said wouldn't go a mile. I had to pay for the others and the mechanic got his head taken off for being so careless as to let me hear his talk.

After days and days more of waiting it was ready. The bill they presented me was staggering——at least three times what I had expected. They explained that the prices were so high on some of the materials used because they had been obliged to get them on the black market. The fantastic labor charge, when I divided it up by the hourly wage, would have paid two experts to work continually for two and a half weeks. I was a fool to pay the bill, but I did. Then I hitched the Alma up to my beloved Ford convertible and took a trial run a few blocks up the road.

I had helper springs and a new clutch installed in my car to be sure it was in good order for pulling. And Fitzhugh had suggested a new type of hitch called a Murat which made for easier riding, backing and maneuvering since the Alma has a rather short tongue. Without the Murat with its two sliding boards between the car and trailer, the car would not be able to turn as much of an angle without bumping the front of the trailer.

When I hauled the trailer down to the spring all went well until I turned to pull alongside the little trailer I was occupying. The sand was softer than I had thought and I got at an angle from which I couldn't move either forward or backward. After studying the situation a minute I saw that by unhitching my car, bringing it around and hitching it again with the car wheels on firmer ground I could put the trailer where I wanted.

A friend had thought she would like to take a jaunt with me and the trailer down to Key West. That smooth level road would be an easy place to become accustomed to trailer hauling. And I had always wanted to see that corner of the country. Folks who knew it well said spring was the loveliest time to take the trip. So, next morning, May 31st, Christie and I started out.

After the uninteresting ride across southern central Florida, we found a good place to park for the night beside Captain Kid's service station near Homewood. The owner was most eager to have us park there, to have us take his picture, and to hook us up to his electricity. Just how many times we put him, his station and his house in darkness that night I don't know, but it is a good thing he had a large supply of fuses. He was still friendly in the morning but I don't think he would have urged us to park with him again on our way back.

The drive down over the Keys was thrilling. The colors were breathtaking and it was a day full of picture taking. We lunched on turtle steaks at Freddie's restaurant in Marathon. Freddie is a pretty little marmoset from Brazil. Christie bought and presented me with a tiny can of choice rattlesnake meat—so frightfully expensive I am still saving it for some ultra special occasion.

We parked the trailer at Hill's auto camp and unhooked the car to run on down and have a look at Key West. On the way we pulled off where a trail led down under one of the long beautiful bridges (one is seven miles long) and had a swim. The water was too warm to be very enjoyable —well over 90 degrees.

After roaming around the quaint old town of Key West and enjoying a glorious sunset after a shower with unforgettable rainbows, we started back for Pirate Cove to dine in a most attractive lodge there.

On the way back, as I rolled along the smooth broad boulevard at 55 or 60 mph, Christie began uneasily eyeing the speedometer. She casually inquired whether I was in any particular hurry to get some place now that the light for pictures was gone.

"No, but why? Are you nervous about this speed on such a fine safe road?" I asked.

"Well," she said, "you know I never drive over 40 and I can't seem to relax and enjoy it when we go any faster."

"But, Christie," I said, "You seemed perfectly happy when we were on our way down with the trailer and you know I went 60 to 65 on some of those long straight stretches."

"Oh, but I feel perfectly safe when I know that big thing is hitched on behind," said Christie.

We hooked up the electricity at Hill's in Marathon. Next morning when Christie turned on the electric stove to make coffee—off went the electricity. It went off for the whole town of Marathon. I walked across the road to where a man was working in his garage and commenting that one of his electric tools seemed to be too much for the power line.

I said nothing but walked back to the trailer and told Christie I thought we'd better use sterno to cook our breakfast. That electric stove they gave me with the trailer looked as though it had seen some rather rough times but they had assured me they had tested it and found it in perfect working order. I decided to give them a little demonstration when I got back.

More nice pictures and a leisurely trip took us back as far as Naples where I thought it would be fun to park near a beautiful beach where we could have a swim in the morning. Even though it was very dark I found the secluded side road leading right down to the beach and pulled in and parked. A few minutes later there was a sharp knock on the door.

"No trailer parking allowed within the town limits," said the officer, "And what's more you've got yourself into something you're not going to be able to get yourself out of. Couldn't you see all this soft sand and the tractor tracks? Even a car can't park here without being pulled out with a tractor."

"I think I can back out," I said.

"I don't think you can," he said, and was gone with, "I'll be back later."

Disappointed at not being allowed to remain in such a lovely spot we locked up the trailer again. It proved to be nothing at all to back out and get onto the hard top road. So there we sat wondering where we'd go to park for the night when the policeman returned. He was so surprised and pleased to find we had got ourselves out without any help his attitude mellowed greatly and he said he knew a very nice place up the road a ways where we could comfortably park for the night. "Just follow me and I'll lead you to it."

On our way back to Sarasota the next day we stopped for one last wonderful swim in my beloved Warm Salt Spring.

When I took the trailer back to Fitzhugh's for a few final details they had not yet finished, I hooked up to their electricity and turned on the stove. More than fuses blew. It was an hour before they had their power again.

They said all they could do would be to trade the old electric stove for a gasoline hot plate. Again I was a sap and came away with a cheap little thing that leaked. Sterno was better.

It was so hot where I parked at the shop, I decided to head up the road and after a pleasant 40-mile drive I found a nice cool quiet cabin resort to stay for the night. With the little experience I'd had, it was quite a feat to maneuver the trailer in among the trees and back it into a parking space where there was barely room to squeeze between a cabin and several large trees.

3. HEADING UP THE COAST

I was grateful for the time I had spent steering, backing, maneuvering and parking a little express wagon when I was a child. The habits formed by playing with that little wagon seemed to make it easier for me to know which way to turn my car to make the trailer back up in the direction I wanted to go.

I soon learned NOT to pay attention to the people with their kind intentions who were apt to be standing about telling me which way to turn the steering wheel. They were almost invariably wrong. I just concentrated on the front wheels of my car and knew that, when backing, the rear end of the trailer would go the direction those front wheels were going. All the help I ever wanted was someone to signal which way the trailer's rear end should go wherever I could not watch the rear end myself.

The next day took me over a bad detour and a stretch of very rough road between Homerville and Waycross. I couldn't go more than 20 miles an hour.

The road was good enough to drive a car 60 or 70 but the slight rolling bumps made the trailer all but turn somersaults. It went up and down like a teeter-totter or a bucking bronco. I tried speed but the faster I went, the worse it got. What a ride! I didn't know a tandem could act like that. The front end of the trailer would go up so high it nearly lifted the rear end of my car right off the ground—and then down with a bang.

Then it did almost as badly on a new cement road with the cracks or seams at even intervals of 30 feet or so. If they'd only make those seams diagonal or make the blocks of concrete a variety of lengths, maybe one wouldn't get into such a rhythm of swinging and swaying.

The trailer rolled best on smooth blacktop, but soon as the sun got high in the sky my radiator began to overheat. I either had to crawl along at about 35 or go 50 for a short time and then stop to let it cool off. I decided the truck drivers who keep up a steady 35 make better time in the end. So I spent the day driving along with one eye on the heat gauge, another scanning the sky in vain for a cloud, and another looking in vain for a shady spot to pull off in. All the best spots seemed to be full of cars or tired cows or signs of cars having been stuck in soft sand.

So it took me from dawn to dark to make 330 miles instead of the easy 600 I would have done with a car alone. I passed only four other trailers heading north. One was crawling around a church yard looking for a shady tree, another was beside the road with the car hood up, and the owners of the other two were pouring cold water in their radiators. Every service station said, "Yeah, it's the same with them all." I was beginning to fear I'd have to admit to an old friend that he was right about not being able to do better than 35 miles an hour except on a trip to Key West.

When I felt tired and wanted to pull off for the night near the little town of Blackshear, Georgia, I saw a house set back from the road. It had a wide level space between the road and a fence so I asked a man who was sprinkling the lawn if I might park there. He invited me to pull in and park away from the road where it would be nice and quiet under the trees in his side yard. He and his wife were so cordial and kind, they refused to take any pay for my parking there in spite of the fact that my trailer wheels tore up a lot of wet sod in their yard when I turned around. I began to think life with a trailer would be very pleasant if I met many more people as hospitable as this Mr. and Mrs. Rhodenberry. I sent them a jar of maple cream from Vermont when I reached home.

It was June 6th and unusually warm. My car overheated and I had to drive slowly or stop occasionally to let it cool off. I covered only 350 miles. At the border between South and North Carolina I pulled off the road, cooked myself a good dinner and rolled into bed at 8:45. I was JUST off the road and the trucks and busses went zooming by all night feeling like earthquakes. I still went to sleep immediately and wondered where I as when I woke up at 5:30 the next morning.

I thought an early start would avoid some of the intense heat but I had to go even slower than the day before because of overheating. After 330 miles I stopped at a gas station just beyond Richmond, Virginia.

After a good night's sleep (it was nice to have my own comfortable bed every night), I headed for Washington, D. C. A heavy rain had cooled things off a bit and I went zipping up and down the high hills north of Richmond. Made it there in two hours.

4. WASHINGTON D.C

I had been told I ought to meet a Mr. McKenney in Washington, D.C. He was running the public relations for most of the trailer dealers' associations. I found that he lived in a trailer park in Alexandria and since I wanted to spend a day in Washington I went there to park.

This particular trailer village was in a horrible location down under some railroad tracks at the outskirts of Alexandria. The heavy rains had flooded half the place. There were hundreds of trailers crowded into the grounds and the only space available for me was off in a far back corner. The minute I backed in and unhitched, a swarm of dirty little brats were climbing all over my car, smearing it with mud, opening and banging my trailer doors, crawling underneath looking for something to twist or turn.

I asked them please go some place else to play. They didn't then I yelled in a loud voice, "You kids please get out of here!" Some of their parents heard but paid no attention.

The views from my windows on both sides were of slopjars, potties, wash-tubs, broken pieces of machinery, tricycles, old tires, wire, bottles and cans and kids being bathed in wash bowls of muddy water. I packed a bag, locked up the trailer, unhitched my car and drove into Washington as fast as I could. Being Sunday I found none of my friends at home but succeeded in getting a room at the Carol Arms.

The next day, after lunching with my friends in the Senate, I looked up McKenney and walked into his office with blood in my eye. I minced no words in telling him just what I thought of his trailer park and told him that now that I had a trailer, by golly, I wasn't going to rest till somebody did something to make things more comfortable and convenient for civilized folks who want to park in attractive surroundings when traveling with a trailer.

He showed me pictures of some parks he considered high class. I thought them all terrible and certainly not what I was looking for. It's a wonder he didn't throw me out of his office.

Then he called in his associate, Bennett who was a photographer and writer, and they kept me there the whole afternoon trying to change my sentiments about trailer parks. McKenney invited me to dine with him in his trailer with his daughter and her husband who were visiting him.

The daughter cooked a delightful meal and I was surely surprised to see what gracious entertaining could be carried on in a trailer.

After dinner, McKenney took me around to show me the development of a new section of the park where they laid out plots in which four trailers might park—one in each corner of the lot with an attractive little square building in the center containing four modern bathrooms. Thus each trailer would have its private bath.

A very large recreation hall was being built and McKenney tried to talk up a lot of advantages in trailer coach living, but I argued that I could see no advantage in having a house on wheels unless it was for travel or frequent moving about. I could readily see, though, that with the housing shortage still so very acute after the war, a trailer might solve the problem of many a young married couple that didn't have a place to live. Even for some families with children, the trailer park provided more fresh air and freedom for the youngsters than some of the crowded sections of the city into which they would otherwise be packed.

There were statistics which tried to show that children in trailer parks were healthier, further advanced in school, and trained in neater and more orderly habits than other children. People living in the amount of space under the ordinary trailer roof would darn well have to cultivate some orderly habits in order to exist at all. And I guess any trailer park, no matter how bad, is better than a city slum. I can readily sympathize with the cities and towns that prohibit trailer parks within their limits, even though there are some very exclusive and elegant trailer parks.

For one with any artistic sense or training in architecture, it would be painful to live where it would be necessary to look out over a group of trailers. The few parks with clean green grass and lots of trees and shrubs with good space between trailers are an improvement, but my idea of the park I would like would be one where, from your trailer, you couldn't possibly see another trailer, no matter which direction you looked.

All that day I kept thinking more and more strongly about a trailer being the thing for me and my work. In the few days I'd had it I could think of more possibilities and opportunities than I had hoped for.

A lot of people are fond of yachts, but they are certainly limited as to where they can go with a boat. And they can't carry a car along for side trips or any fun on land. And think what yachts cost! To me a trailer could be as comfortable and attractive as any yacht and if you like water you can go and park beside it.

On they way north from Washington D. C., the generator quit working, the battery was down and the radiator kept overheating, especially going through Baltimore. When I stopped there for gas, I very foolishly took the radiator cap off. Luckily I was wearing my old Panama hat which kept the scalding water and steam from my face, but I had slipped my hands into a pair of cotton work gloves and my hands got painfully burned. All the fingers of my right hand and thumb and first finger of my left were blistered. Obtundia deadened the pain but it wasn't easy to drive with greasy hands. I went on with a pretty big lump in my throat.

The temperature dropped as I headed into New York City. I spent the next few days with business and pleasure dates in town. I spent a delightful evening with the Driscols in Yonkers. I told my friend Charlie that I thought it would be interesting to use the trailer to gather picture and story material from Key West to Alaska. I told him I was thinking of a photo assignment to Liberia first and then prepare for an Alaskan adventure the following spring.

"To hell with Liberia," said Charlie, "Alaska is much more vital interest to us all right now. Go there first—this summer."

5. PACKING FOR ALASKA

On into Brattleboro, Vermont without anything else going wrong. But I knew there would be no use trying to get the trailer up the terribly steep rough road to my farm, so I parked it at the Ford garage.

I was extremely fond of my Ford convertible and it was doing quite nicely with its heavy truck clutch. That clutch had really stood a lot of abuse without damaging it. But I just didn't have enough power on hills.

Having seen the trouble the average passenger car has pulling anything except the very smallest, lightest trailers, I decided I was facing a problem. If I wanted to load my trailer with a lot of heavy equipment and undertake anything like a trip over the Alaska Highway I'd need something with a helluva a lot more pulling ability than an ordinary car.

Leaving my farm in Putney, Vermont, August 1947

I had a great respect for jeeps after the day I was pulled out of an embarrassing predicament with the burned out clutch in Washington. Most of my friends who had had anything to do with them in the army said they were so uncomfortable I wouldn't survive many miles of travel

in one and that in a cold country I'd surely freeze to death.

I did not want to haul my trailer with a big truck. I kept thinking of all the running around I'd be wanting to do hunting and fishing and it seemed hard to imagine getting dressed up to go to a formal affair in a truck. A jeep I could see going absolutely anywhere.

The very next day after pulling my trailer into Brattleboro, a dealer from down country brought a jeep into my Ford garage to sell. It was very cute looking, especially without the top, its gray color matching my trailer exactly. Mr. Bemis told me to take it and use it until I had given it a good try-out. Within a couple of days I decided to buy it.

When I hooked onto the trailer to pull it to the farm, I had a devil of a time where I had to shift into tractor low on the long steep curving hill toward Putney. I held up a long line of traffic. Then I found that without any weight in the jeep I couldn't keep all four wheels firmly enough on the ground to make the last lap of the 27 percent grade of the very bad road leading to my house. I called a friend who had a jeep and with his help the two jeeps brought the trailer up into the yard where I wanted to park.

No one around here knew anything about the jeep. It had a 3000-watt 110-volt AC generator and a rather compact air cooled four-cylinder motor made of light aluminum. It was designed for some war use.

It seemed advisable to have a whole new and heavier wiring system installed in the trailer since its wires were so light they would not be safe for heavy loads of photographic equipment, heaters, and cooking.

I was determined to use electricity for cooking and persuaded Mr. Fitzhugh that I'd been given a pretty raw deal on buying a trailer with an electric stove and coming away with a cheap little gasoline hot plate. He agreed to send me a good electric stove and did. It would have been foolish to start out for the remote parts with the butane stove with which most trailers are equipped. It is impossible to get bottled gas in many out-of-the way places. And I do not consider gasoline stoves safe, especially if a trailer is to be pounded over rough roads. There have been disastrous results from unnoticed leaks caused by vibrating tanks or pipes.

Electric stoves and heaters present problems when hooking up in some trailer parks. Not many parks have large enough fuses and some have such low voltage you may have difficulty getting heat enough to cook a meal. I knew I'd better carry along a good supply of 30-amp fuses.

I was told it might be hard to get kerosene or fuel oil to use in the trailer heater in some areas. I put all my hopes for comfort, safety and convenience in my electric plant. After all, I couldn't go anywhere without gas and gas would give me electricity as long as my light plant continued to work efficiently.

I moved things into the trailer, I moved them out, I moved others in, I juggled and arranged and rearranged. I slept in it and cooked and ate in it most of the time. I wanted to become thoroughly accustomed to it and find out what furnishings and equipment would be most satisfactory to have in the trailer.

I wanted to be set up for housekeeping anytime and all the time so I figured out ways of fastening or fixing things right on the shelves or wherever they belonged so that they would not slide around or fall off. I had wire racks to hold what dishes were kept on open shelves. Of course the shelves had little moldings or risers at the edges.

I had a system of straps which held a lot of things in place, such as the radio, my photo enlarger, and other equipment. I fastened little things called foot loops on the walls and slipped the straps through. The risers on the book case shelves seemed to keep books from falling out, but I added a strap to the shelf holding the big Webster International and a few other heavy books.

When my son came to visit me, he said my work on the trailer reminded him of what the navy called conditioning a ship before embarking on a voyage. He helped me wax the outside. This kept dust and dirt from sticking and made it easier to clean.

Instead of using the kitchen for a dark room as I first planned, I decided eating was too important a business to crowd and clutter up the kitchen. I wanted to be able to step in and get a meal as quickly and easily as possible, especially when on the road.

I made a large desk and lab work table in the living room by having a plywood top resting on four filing cabinets, two at each end. In order to keep things as light as possible I bought pasteboard filing cabinets. I painted the whole thing gray and it really wasn't too bad looking.

I wanted as many seats as possible but dispensed with one of the chairs and replaced it with a box with a padded top to carry my photo chemical bottles.

Guatemala materials made attractive drapes and I lined them with two layers of black satin so they could shut out the light enough to do dark room work.

When some friends called one afternoon they caught me walking across the lawn in a sun suit carrying my skis. I had to pack everything for both winter and summer, as well as all the in between times and be prepared for any and all occasions. Of course I wanted all my hunting and fishing equipment. The closets and drawers began to get stuffed and I just hoped that what I needed first would be on top.

I tried out picture printing in the trailer and it all worked very well. Then I felt I was pretty well set to start at last for Alaska. It was still necessary at that time to obtain a permit in Edmonton to travel the highway from Dawson Creek north. I certainly did not want to get as far as Edmonton, away off up in Alberta, and then find I would not be allowed to proceed further. But there was no way to obtain any guarantee of a permit.

Everyone had to submit to examination of car and travelling equipment there in Edmonton in order to secure the permit. There were many rules, regulations and requirements for travel over the Alaska Highway. One had to carry a long list of spare parts for the car. I had quite a time getting all those many, many parts for the jeep but the dealer finally brought them up from Massachusetts.

When Mr. McKenney came over again to give it all a last inspection, he crawled underneath the trailer and discovered a very bad situation. It was a very weak-looking metal frame and the welds at the front end were all broken loose. A man came out and welded a few places and then I towed it gingerly down to Brattleboro where he did a lot more welding and reinforcing. He also built a rack to carry two extra tires on the front end of the jeep.

6. HEADED WEST AT LAST

In the early morning of September 1, 1947 I started out by the light of the full harvest moon— propitious, according to the old timers. A slow but pleasant climb up and down Hogback and other high points of the Molly Stark Trail probably took me almost as long as it took Molly Stark. My jeep went up the steep grades so slowly the speedometer hardly registered. Then the muffler fell apart. I'm afraid I woke everyone living anywhere near the road from Wilmington into Bennington where I had to sit and wait a couple of hours for a garage to open and have the thing welded.

I was routing myself through Ontario and then over through Michigan in order to stop at Fitzhugh's to have some more work done. There were several things needing attention. For example, the hot water heater they had installed in Florida never did work right and nearly blew up several times.

Fitzhugh had suggested that I come there to his company's home office where, in his big garage, he had good men and facilities for fixing everything right. He said he would build a cage covering for the light plant in the jeep to protect it and make better storage space around it for

Colfax, Wisconsin.
Where my Grandfather Mathews pulled up in a covered wagon

Colfax, Wisconsin. My grandfather pulled up to this very spot with his oxen and covered wagon in 1860.

extra gas cans, tires, hoses, tools, spare parts, etc. I knew I'd have to acquire more gas cans for the Alaskan trip.

I went into Canada over the Livingston Bridge. The customs officials only seemed interested in my photographic equipment and were evidently unaccustomed to really good cameras and enlargers. They were flabbergasted at the values. When the inspector brought in his figures the officer at the desk told him he must have made a mistake and calmly dropped off a 0 when filling out the forms I was to turn in at the other end.

At Fitzhugh's I parked in their big trailer repair shop, not exactly a pleasant place to be living in the heat. There was very little air at night when they closed all the windows. A giant air compressor went on and off all night; it was much worse than the Potomac Freight Yards. Since I got there on a Saturday they didn't accomplish much that afternoon, but Fitzhugh said they'd have me out by Monday night.

After five miserable days there I went to pieces and got a room at a hotel.

I never saw such incompetent workmen! I watched two men who called themselves plumbers replace the hot water heater and put in a shower — a very simple installation. They didn't even know how to cut and solder copper pipe and made a terrible mess of both jobs. They had to take them apart time and time again to fix the joints and connections which continued to leak. When I saw the shower faucet handles at a cock-eyed angle they told me they were not an adjustable type.

"Hand me a screw driver," I said in disgust and immediately set them right myself. And when I called Fitzhugh's attention to a pipe which was still leaking he said, "Oh, that one is in a closet where it won't matter."

I found out later that they got the shower fixtures at Sears Roebuck down the street and let me have them at a very large profit. Then they took out the water heater which their Florida shop had installed. It was no good. A whole miserable week passed before I finally got away from that dreadful place leaving altogether too much of my money behind me.

I wanted to go over through northern Wisconsin and surprise some cousins on a farm near Colfax. I thought the ferry from Ludington across Lake Michigan to Manitowoc would be a pleasant ride and save a lot of mileage. I found the rate for an outfit like mine terribly high, something over $40.

Every time I cross Lake Michigan it seems to be in a storm, and oh how the wind from the north can get rolling down the length of the old lake. This night was terrible. I knew my only way to survive would be to remain out on deck in the open air. I had taken a state room in the hope of getting some sleep but when I saw what was happening to everyone else I cleared out. The big boat was crowded and the faces were all turning green and gray almost before we pulled away from the Michigan shore.

I later found that the things in my trailer got more of a tossing around than they ever did on the roughest of roads.

It was just dusk when I pulled into my cousins' farm and they weren't as surprised as I had hoped since a notice had come from the Post Office asking whether they knew an Iris Woolcock.

I got a thrill out of pulling my trailer up on the very spot my grandfather and grandmother drew up their covered wagon in 1860 to pioneer among the Indians in the wilderness. It wasn't very long before they had 1200 acres of wheat. It wasn't easy work but they had courage and confidence and I remember my grandmother well enough to know what wonderful spirit she met and overcame all obstacles. She was one of the few among the white settlers there who were able to make friends of the Indians. As a child I enjoyed her stories of those early days. That is probably one reason why I wanted to see the pioneering people of today in Alaska.

My cousins had a lovely place for me to park on their side lawn under the trees.

When I was pulling out the doorstep I noticed a pipe sticking out under the trailer with a valve on it. I hadn't watched everything done by those hopelessly inefficient old gents the Fitzhugh organization called plumbers, but I remembered telling them the water heater would have to have some means of draining it should the trailer ever be left without heat in cold weather. They had said they'd put a drain pipe in the bottom.

So this was what they had done! They had put a pipe into the bottom of the tank, and with many elbows and joins led it out underneath the trailer. Then they put a valve on the end out near the side of the trailer.

They were very thoughtful about my not being obliged to crawl underneath very far in order to open and close the valve. Did it ever dawn upon them that that long piece of pipe and valve out in the open under the trailer would always be full of water? And that a pipe full of water would not need to go as far as Alaska to freeze in the open air of a Michigan or a Vermont winter? All that was needed was a small piece of pipe just long enough to go through the floor of the trailer with a valve above the floor inside the trailer beside the tank where there was plenty of room.

So I had to take the trailer over to the blacksmith in Colfax. Ernest Haugle had been blacksmithing, welding, plumbing and fixing the farmers' machinery there for many years, and as did his father before him. He was a popular fellow and I am not surprised. It was good to meet a man who KNEW his trade, was an expert at it, and proud of it.

When he looked at my water heater connections he said he didn't think whoever put them together had ever done any plumbing. He brazed some copper and brass together and made a nice new fitting and what a pleasure it was to watch him work. He charged me a dollar. Think what I had to pay those dumb, DUMB dumbbells who took hours and hours to do the job and do it all wrong to the tune of $2.50 per hour each.

7. A FARMING LESSON

(Iris headed out for the west, passing through Rochester, Minnesota to visit the Mayo Clinic to see if anything could be done for her migraine headaches. No promising results. Then it was through Fargo, Grand Forks and Minot, North Dakota. By the time she came to Culbertson, Montana...)

I was so thrilled with those vast stretches of flat open prairie I wanted to live right there about a week to get the real feel of it.

(Soon she found an abandoned farm where she could park her trailer. It wasn't long before she knew everyone and everyone knew her. She was offered tours around the countryside and heard many stories from the locals. And she soon formulated some opinions about what was going on around this part of the country.)

The "strip farming" method of raising wheat presented beautiful patterns for pictures, especially after the wheat had been harvested leaving the strips of golden stubble alternating with the strips of clean, rich dark brown soil. I soon learned, however, that the land which looked so pretty was not being farmed correctly according to the opinions of those who had seriously studied what was best for the land in the long run.

Driving into Culbertson, one day after getting my mail I noticed a new building with "Extension Service" in gold letters over the door. I walked in, met the county agent, Don Hunter, and told him I was very interested in finding out how the Extension Service operated out there since I had spent a year working with them in New Hampshire, Maine and Vermont. I wanted to know what some of the problems of the wheat country were and told him I would be glad to offer my services gratis if he could use a photographer for a day and let me go around with him or any of the other Extension Service people to take some pictures they could use. He was delighted, saying they were much in need of pictures for their annual bulletin and found it difficult if not impossible to secure any of the sort they needed.

The following three days were packed full of extremely interesting work for me. I learned a lot and was never thrown with any finer, more intelligent young men than those I met here.

Soil conservation was, of course, of major importance there. We may some day greatly regret that anyone ever tried to grow wheat in Montana. It might have been much better to have left it all in grassland. The farmer who has plowed up his land either does not know with what speed his topsoil is disappearing, or else he does not care. In most cases, if he can do well with his crops for a few years he is not bothering his head about the next generation and does NOT want to be told what to do or what not to do with his land. He owns it and thinks he has a right to do what he damn well pleases with it regardless of what harm his practices may do to his neighbor or to the community or to the world.

So I learned that those clean strips of land lying between the stubble —those strips which looked nice to me and of which Scottie and other farmers were so proud—those strips were very BAD, according to the soil conservation boys. Those beautiful plowed and harrowed fields were losing all their topsoil, and fast. It was all blowing away. I took pictures of great drifts of it like snow piled up along fences and roads. In dry spells it is worse, of course, making the dreadful dust storms. The boys explained that much of the most valuable part of that topsoil is very light and once it gets whirled up by the wind it is not caught along the fences in the drifts but keeps on flying, probably out over the Atlantic Ocean. At the rate it is going now it will not be so very long before it is all gone.

If what they call a Noble Blade, a type of machine made and very successfully used in Canada, could be more widely introduced in Montana, it would help save some of the topsoil. It is a blade that slides under the surface just deep enough to cut and kill the roots of the weeds. It leaves all the dead weeds, stubble and "trash," as they call it, lying on top, holding the moisture and keeping the soil from blowing away, and also acting as shade and protection for the young seedling plants.

The farmers object to this type of farming because their farms do not look as nice and also because it takes some practice to operate this blade properly, though it takes less time to keep the ground in shape than by their other methods.

Farmers always seem to be the hardest type of people to convince of any new and better methods and if you quote any soil conservation or Extension Service facts or figures to a man like Scottie he will say, "Yeah, those young fellers out of eastern colleges can do their farming on paper. I'll do mine on the land." Another bad drought such as they had from about '32 through '36 will make him pay more attention.

A little to the west of McCabe there was a colony of Russian farmers and it was interesting to see how their methods differed. They did not put all their eggs in one basket but carried on a more general farming.

Instead of rotating with fallow strips they planted corn between the plots of wheat. The yield of wheat was slightly less but they more than made up for it through their corn and pigs. Then they all had their beef and dairy cattle, chickens, vegetables and anything and everything else they could raise. They couldn't make a killing on their wheat as did some of the others in good years and close up the house and go to Florida for the winter, but when it came to a poor wheat year they were a lot more secure.

After pulling out of McCabe I stopped over a couple of days in Culbertson to spend more time with my soil conservation and Extension Service friends. These were certainly swell types of fine, healthy, good looking, extremely alert young people, heart and soul interested in their work. They sincerely LOVE the land. They do so want to see it handled to the best of their knowledge and capabilities. They firmly believe that there can be no world peace unless everyone gets enough to eat. They feel that this country has been and is being so wasteful of its resources and that much of the burden of feeding the world will be on our hands because of the ever increasing population and the fact that in all of densely populated Europe there is so little land left fit for raising food.

I had three little bums for company... lambs whose ewes had deserted them.

8. A MAJOR DETOUR

It was really cold when I left Culbertson. I rode along with the light plant going so that the electric steam radiator would keep the trailer warm. The heat from the light plant motor running behind me in the jeep kept me so nice and warm I had the windshield open most of the time.

Everyone guessed that I was going to Alaska with those red gas cans plastered all over the jeep. The chap who ran the hardware store in Glasgow was all for going right along with me. He had spent a lot of time in Alaska during the war. He gave me a note to a friend of his in Fairbanks. I had such a list of people to say hello to by then that I could have done nothing else for weeks. I had an equally long list of people who wanted me to let them know how I had found things up there since they were planning to go up before long.

The last time I had whirled out over Route 2, it had seemed easy to cover six or seven hundred miles a day. Now I was covering about 150 miles a day. The road still looked level but it was a steady climb and the jeep was so slow.

The radio was telling of snow every place else, a 30-inch fall with roads blocked further south. The sky was dark with heavy clouds but as I looked to the southwest of Harlem, I caught my breath when I saw a streak of silver sunshine on some high snow-covered mountain peaks piercing the clouds — the Rockies! They looked formidable but were only foothills, the Bear Paw Range.

Most of the Indians I had met in Culbertson had looked glum and sullen and just stared, but every Indian I met along the road out here had a great big smile and a wave for me.

A typical sight would be an Indian driving a crazy looking team of one tiny horse and one tall, lanky horse, hitched all skewgee to a crookedly old wagon with wheels sprawling in all directions and a long-legged colt following down the road.

Sometimes a couple of Indian boys would be loping along on horse-back rounding up a small herd of cattle or wild horses. In Indian farmhouse was usually made of logs and mud, had a yard full of junk and countless dogs and a number of horses feeding at a haystack nearby.

When I reached Havre I was told there was only one place to park trailers, a gas station on the west end of town. It was managed by a nice couple, Jim and Rose Scrivens. They were stopping over on their way to Alaska to homestead. Their homemade truck-house had broken its rear axle so many times they decided to stop over in Havre long enough to rebuild it. While working on the truck, they got the job of running the gas station for the winter and had strung a few electric cords out to half a dozen trailers. But Jim said there wasn't enough juice to run stoves or heaters.

It was pretty cold my first night there and since I couldn't use their electricity for heat I kept the oil stove going. But it wasn't enough to keep the pump from freezing. So next morning I had to hook up to my power plant and use the electric heaters to thaw out the pump. Then I took the bed out (anything but an easy job) and packed a lot of insulating material between the pump and the rear corner of the trailer. I found a leak between the pump and the pressure tank. It was evident that it had been leaking a long time but was easy to fix by merely tightening a nut.

Then I chased all over town and finally found enough flexible fiber hose to try to pipe the heat from the oil heater back to the rear of the trailer. After I fussed for hours getting it rigged up it didn't work right. The heat wouldn't go back far enough. Either the blower wasn't strong enough or else the floor was so cold it blocked the heat. The floor was so cold that if I took off wet or snowy shoes, they'd freeze and stick tight to the floor.

I had to resort to using my own light plant to get enough heat and I had a terrible time starting it in the cold. It just wouldn't run well and went from bad to worse using a terrific amount of oil. After several days it refused to run at all.

I was told there was a bright young G.I. mechanic named Jim Scriven in one of the garages who liked to tinker with light plants so I went to see him. He shook his tousled head of blonde curls when he found the light plant frozen, i.e. stuck fast. With some penetrating oil and a lot of elbow grease he finally got it going. It didn't sound at all healthy. The boy was fearful of its condition inside so I told him to go ahead and take it apart and find out what was really wrong.

When Fitzhugh had built the cage over the plant he had not thought of leaving any possible way of getting in to examine the carburetor or spark plugs or to make any adjustments. The whole thing had to be disassembled from the bottom up.

Then taking the light plant apart was SOMETHING. I had no idea how complicated it was inside and neither did the boy. In order to get the crank shaft out the whole darn generator had to be taken apart. He found the crank shaft badly worn. I looked at the billion parts covering the workbench, a table and half the garage floor and wondered how in heavens name anyone could EVER get them all back together again.

Since Jim was a pretty good mechanic I set him fixing the clearance lights on the trailer.

Then he went to work on the oil heater to see whether he could do anything about that. It looked as though a thorough cleaning might help. It proved to be a horribly impractical thing to take apart. The things which might need attention more or less frequently were so placed that the whole stove had to come out and be disassembled in order to get at them.

And I was learning how very important it was to have the stove absolutely level in order for it to run at all. There was no possible way of leveling the stove in the trailer. Therefore, the trailer had to be parked perfectly level. If trailer manufacturers would only travel a few miles with a trailer and park one a couple of times they might learn a few things.

Fitzhugh had told me this heater had scarcely been used since the people who owned the trailer had occupied it only a couple of weeks right down there in Florida where it was warm. But we found it a terrible mess of burned and caked carbon with some parts nearly rusted through. I thought those must have been a rather strenuous two weeks that this trailer was supposedly used.

When Jim got the heater together again it worked a little better but, at best, it sure was a poor heating system. You might fry an egg on the ceiling over the stove without being able to melt an ice cube anywhere on the floor. I fastened a little electric fan to the ceiling over the stove and that helped a little but not nearly enough.

I was beginning to grow more and more worried about how I could get along in this outfit without freezing to death further north. After all, I was headed for a helluva lot colder weather than I could ever experience in Havre, Montana.

When I went into the phone office to call my friend Mac one day he was at a convention in Philadelphia. After a long wait, the operator said, "That's Philadelphia, Massachusetts, isn't it?"

I told Mac that the oil stove had been taken apart again and repaired and that my shoes were still freezing to the floor and water pipes were freezing. I knew I could go no further north without having another floor built underneath the trailer. I would also have to buy enough carpet to completely cover the floor inside and come up a ways around the walls.

He said to hold on before spending any more money on that old jalopy and let him see what some trailer manufacturers would do for me with an eye to what good publicity might come out of my travels.

Mac suggested several makes he knew which had heated floors. When he called back later, he asked me where I'd rather go to pick up a new trailer, Los Angeles or Bremen, Indiana.

I had heard so many good things about the Westcraft Company in California that I wanted very much to have one of their trailers, but Mac said they told him they could not have one of their new models with bath ready for me in less than two months. The Liberty Company in Indiana was turning out a thirty-three foot model with bath and said it would not take more than a week after my arrival there to run one off their assembly line with any changes or special installations I might want. They told Mac they would let me have it at cost and take my old one off my hands if I could not dispose of it elsewhere.

I tried to sell it in Montana but had no good offers for it. I thought, anyway, it would be just as well to take it along to Indiana so that I could have my electric pump and possibly the water heater removed and put in the new trailer.

There were a few other light plants like mine around that section of the country, none of them proving satisfactory. I also found that my friend, Fitzhugh, had charged me about a hundred dollars more for it than they had been selling for anywhere else at retail.

Jim was always pointing out my jeep and trailer to his customers telling them about my going to Alaska. When a man who had supervised one of the construction crews when the highway was being built came along, I stuck my head out just in time to hear him say, "Hrumpf, I certainly don't advise a woman to undertake that trip alone."

After I talked with him for five minutes he grabbed my hand and shook it enthusiastically, saying "Sure, YOU'LL make it—only wish I

Appliance show, Havre, Montana. All the latest conveniences for the farm family.

were going with you." Then he said the worst that could happen would be that I might run into a big drift across one of the cuts and be stuck two or three days But after looking over my equipment he said, "You'll know how to take care of yourself."

I told him I knew there would be plenty of wood up there and if it came to the worst I could make a stove out of my big lard can and let the smoke out through a ventilator in the top of the trailer. He said, "You'll find a lot of people living up there in tents or sheet metal huts without a stove or even a hole in the roof to let the smoke out."

A detour of about 4000 miles to change trailers, light plants, etc. now lay between me and the Alaska Highway. But the reports of the condition of the highway grew worse as more travelers came down.

A car stopped with three fellows—two asleep in the back seat. The driver said they'd been taking turns driving without any stopovers and that they were all nervous wrecks after seven days and nights of the worst ice they'd ever driven over. It seems there was still little or no snow up there and some occasional slight thawing which kept the ice smooth and glary. There were countless trucks wrecked or in ditches or stalled on nearly every hill. This driver said he'd prefer extreme cold to ice any day and I knew I would too. He said later in the winter it would get so cold that even if there should be any ice it would become granular and no longer slippery.

I figured the detour back to Indiana and Michigan would occupy a good deal of time but allow me to get back and up the highway sometime in late January or early February at the latest. Then the good winter road would still be at its best. I wanted to see that north country in winter as well as in summer and thought I might make the return trip the following spring or early summer as soon as the mud conditions dried up.

I soon learned that I'd just better quit trying to make any plans where the element TIME was concerned.

9. SECOND THOUGHTS

As for getting permits to travel the highway from Edmonton, it became evident that there were occasions when permits were denied. A man pulled into the station to stop overnight. He was with the Standard Oil Company and said he and a big outfit were on their way to Alaska but had been denied permits. What tales he told!

He was absolutely certain that NO travel was allowed over the Alaska Highway. He insisted it had been abandoned and was completely impassable. He just wouldn't believe us when we told him cars were driving though from Anchorage or Fairbanks every day or so. No, he knew better. He said a big crew from the oil company who had been working for 18 months up near Dawson City were in bad need of a vacation. He and a bunch of fellows from Texas and Louisiana had been sent up to relieve the crews. He said now they weren't being allowed to go up and the fellows there were not being allowed to come down.

Then he went on with great tales of all the bridges being washed out, never to be rebuilt, and the highway itself all caving in. "Why there won't be any road left up there within about six months. I KNOW. Our company is in on the ground floor with everything up there."

Late the next night a car rolled in having averaged 500 miles a day from Fairbanks with no trouble whatsoever. The driver said that snow was falling and the road was less slippery and he needed to use chains only once.

Sometimes I weakened on the idea of returning to change trailers and I tried to figure out more things that might be done to the old one to make it do. Many of the water pipes would have to be moved to warmer parts of the trailer. And the oil stove was carrying me past the stage of anger. It had brought me to the point where I just sat down and cried. It was forever going out, flooding, smoking, refusing to start, using up box after box of matches. Another trailer with the same stove also had loads of trouble.

In spite of all these things, I was still fond of my trailer and with the feeling of loyalty I had for it and all the work I had put into making it attractive and comfortable, I hated to think of changing.

But some decision had to be made and made without any more delay. I got another call from Mac and he advised me to definitely make the change to a better and warmer trailer before going further north. Then I called Fitzhugh to tell him my predicament and he said if I would bring both the trailer and light plant back to Indiana or Michigan, he was sure he could sell them for me.

As usual, he did some suave talking and why I was dumb enough to have the least atom of confidence in a single word he said, I don't know.

Mac called again and invited me to Detroit to spend the holidays with him and his son's family where I could easily connect with Fitzhugh, contact the light plant manufacturer and possibly change the jeep for a Dodge power wagon or something that would have more speed and power.

Heading back toward the east on Route 2 was a bit easier than going west; that slight downgrade helped the little old jeep enough for me to roll along at about 50 mph and the small part of the afternoon which was left after I finally got away from Havre was enough to reach Glasgow that evening.

(Iris headed for Jackson, Michigan, passing through Minneapolis and Chicago en route for her showdown with Fitzhugh.)

10. "HE'D CHEAT HIS OWN MOTHER."

I pulled off near an office at the edge of town where Fitzhugh would be sure to find me. He came along a few minutes later and so did a car with two cops to tell me I couldn't park there. Fitzhugh showed them his card and gave them some big talk about what an important guy he was and tried to make them think I was important too. "Why that trailer of hers is worth $5000 and I'm here to negotiate a trade with her," he said.

His big talk got him nowhere with the officers. I tried to get a word in but he wasn't going to let me. I finally went around to the other side of their car and said, "Listen, officers, this is my business. If you don't wish me to park here I'll be glad to move on. I would appreciate being allowed to park here for the night since it is so late. But if it is against the law maybe you could suggest where I might look for a place." One of them said quietly, "You can stay right here." And then off they drove.

Then I said to Fitzhugh, "If you consider my trailer worth $5000, how much are you going to give me for it?"

He came into the trailer, very grandiosely opening a package he brought me as a Christmas present — a barometer to hang on the trailer wall. Would he buy the trailer and the electric plant? Would he make some sort of offer for them? Oh no, he couldn't do that. He'd be willing to take them and try to sell them for me. He didn't know how soon he'd be able to move them. Trailers weren't selling very fast right now and as for the light plant, there might not be a call for a thing like that for some time. Maybe next summer someone would be able to use it in a camp upstate.

He couldn't make any down payment on them and, of course, there could be no guarantee as to how soon he might be able to sell them.

So, that was how far I got with him. Was I blue!

Mac had a friend who was a trailer dealer nearby and he let me pull my trailer into his parking lot. Mac had told him about my wanting to sell my trailer and when I drove in with it, without looking inside of it, and just giving the outside a casual glance, he said, "Did you say this was a 1946 Alma?"

"Yes," I said, "that's what the bill of sale says." Then I told him about getting it from Fitzhugh in June of '47 who claimed it was a late '46 used only two weeks before I got it.

The dealer shook his head and said he'd been handling Almas for a long time and he knew mine was not a '46.

I had noticed a serial number of a "skip" listed by Fitzhugh in a trailer magazine a few weeks before. A skip is a trailer that rolls off without being paid for. This one was listed as a '46 but with a serial number so much higher than mine that I thought the Alma Company would scarcely have been able to turn out that many trailers in a year.

Then another incident made me suspicious when a woman in the Rochester trailer park had told me my trailer looked just like the '44 Alma her mother had had so much trouble with because of its wartime construction.

When I saw Fitzhugh and asked him whether he was sure mine was a '46 he had said yes, of course, and told me there was no difference in them during those years. They all looked alike.

I wired my serial number to the Alma factory. The reply telegram read: ALMA TRAILER MODEL 90-323 SOLD AUGUST 11, 1944 TO MACDONALD TRAILER SALES AT DETROIT. TRAILER PAID FOR AT TIME OF DELIVERY.

I wrote Fitzhugh. No reply. I wired. Finally a telegram came stating that he had the original bill of sale showing the Alma had sold new in '45 and that there was "no change in models '45 and '46." He completely ignored the fact that it was a '44.

I phoned him and asked him whether he realized the seriousness of what he had done and told him I would bring suit against him unless he helped me out of my predicament with this old trailer at once. He said he'd let me know.

No word. I wired again asking for an immediate yes or no reply as to whether he would pay $3000 cash for the trailer and light plant. That was about half as much than I had paid him. This would surely have left him off easy. His reply came back: WE HAVE A LARGE INVENTORY AT PRESENT AND NO CAN DO.

So I filed away his bills and letters after having photostat copies made of the most important ones to send to a lawyer to keep for the time when I could start the legal proceedings.

I found that Fitzhugh was pretty well known around those parts and when people would learn of some of the atrocities he perpetrated on me, they would usually say, "Oh, Fitzhugh WOULD do a thing like that." One man who had dealt with him for years and knew his family said, "Raymond Fitzhugh is so crooked he'd cheat his own mother — in fact I've known him to do just that."

Now the only thing left to do was to throw myself on the mercy of someone else in the hope that I wouldn't be taken for another ride. With Mac's kind and helpful advice I felt a bit easier, but I was beginning to wonder just how much confidence I ought to place in anyone. Yet I still wanted a trailer in spite of all the trials and tribulations I had suffered.

11. WHAT THEY WON'T DO TO A WOMAN

Mac was extremely loyal to the trailer industry and he was hoping I might help give it a boost. He put in the entire week in Detroit paying attention to nothing but my problems, seeing people and making phone calls galore.

Mac went to work to help me get a new Kohler light plant and before I knew it all arrangements were made for me to pick up one from a dealer in Detroit.

Getting rid of my old light plant was not so easy. The people from whom it came finally told me they would buy it. I was grateful for the fact that Mac was present when they made the arrangement. When I want back to deliver it to them alone, they went back on their word and refused to pay me as much as they promised. I had nothing else to do with the old plant but take it out of the jeep and leave it with them. I had to go after the new Kohler and the jeep couldn't hold TWO light plants. I was sure Mac could make them come across with the payment and he finally did, but not for several months. If he had not been in on it from the start to help me out, I'd probably still be waiting for the check.

What they won't do to a woman!

Mac tried to cheer me up about the trailer by telling me Spencer, president and owner of the Liberty Coach Company, was his friend, his real friend, and he knew he would allow me the new one at cost with a liberal trade in on the old one.

12. WITH LIBERTY AND JUSTICE

The Liberty Coach Company had three factories in Indiana: one in Bremen, one in Wakarusa, and one in Syracuse, all within a radius of about twenty miles. The one at Syracuse had recently burned and they were planning soon to give up Wakarusa and carry on all their business at Bremen in an elaborate new plant they were planning to build there.

The company was very much a one man affair. H.L. Spencer owned it and bossed it and HE was BOSS. He drew his family affairs into it to a considerable extent by having most of his relatives on his staff. He was a big gambler, having splurged a few times before and gone broke. He was a personality and I could see the minute I saw him that he would be someone interesting to watch, and as I found out later, to watch out for.

I went out with Mac to the Wakarusa plant to see the big 33-foot Libertys rolling through the assembly line. The smaller jobs were being turned out in Bremen. They had been doing twenty 33-footers a day but business was slacking off.

I was interested in seeing every step in construction and we went back first to the beginning of the line where the metal frames were brought in. That underneath structure was so very important to me. The frames were being made for them by a metal shop in Elkhart.

Mac thought they looked very good. They looked a lot better than what I had seen underneath the old Alma. The wide pieces of channel iron LOOKED heavy. I didn't like the short pieces of the tongue which went back under the front end and told Mac I thought they might break where they were fastened to the rest of the frame. He pooh-poohed me with "Why that's welded. It can't break." I thought to myself, "But welds DO break."

However I kept still, thinking that a mere woman shouldn't say too much. When we got down to the finished trailers they looked very lovely inside and I was thrilled at the idea of having one. I began to plan how I could arrange it for my photo lab work. Mr. Spencer's son was supervising the production of these 33-foot jobs and I was told to give him a little diagram of any changes I might want made in the arrangement of closets, cupboards, shelves, etc.

They called that model a six-passenger trailer. It had the bedroom with double bed in rear. In front of that came a hall with the bathroom on one side and two bunk beds on the other side, then the kitchen, and finally the living room in the front end with either a studio couch or a love seat which would open out into a double bed.

I decided to leave out the bunk beds and use that space for my dark room in conjunction with the running water in the bathroom. I figured I could wash small prints or film in the wash bowl and large prints in a tub. There was a light-tight sliding door at the bathroom and at each end of this center bedroom. Where the bunk beds had been planned they built a good solid cabinet workbench for me, low enough to give plenty of head room for my enlarger. It was right over the wheel housing, thereby giving a good steady place for the enlarger to ride the rough roads. Underneath there was plenty of storage space for chemical bottles, an electric dryer, cutting board, and loads of other things.

When Spencer's son, Allen, showed me the various pieces of equipment in one of the finished trailers, he said the toilet was electric. I didn't see how one could work electrically, noticed no wires, and it looked like the hydraulic motor garbage disposal toilet affair I had in my old trailer. Oh no, he insisted it was electric.

Well, I thought that must be an improvement. I didn't know that to Allen the word motor just automatically meant something electrical. The word hydraulic was not in his vocabulary.

Then he said they were going to put a new type of stove, a Harrison stove, in my trailer because they were better than any other trailer stove made. He said it would be ideal for me going off into remote places because I could burn any one of three fuels in it - oil, bottled gas, or gasoline. I told him that would be wonderful.

I wouldn't want bottle gas since I was sure I wouldn't be able to get it up in the far north, but I said it was certainly a clever idea to have a stove in which you could burn either oil or gasoline.

I couldn't for the life of me figure out how such a combination might be rigged up and asked him several times whether he was SURE I'd be

having a stove which would burn gasoline or oil. He always said yes. Liberty Then one day when I saw him sitting across the hotel dining room with Coach several other men I thought might know something about stoves I called Factory, out, "Allen, do you still think that stove will run on either gasoline, Breman, butane, or oil?" Allen said, "That's what they told me." The men roared Indiana. and Allen's face got red.

They were calling this 33-foot model with bath "Allen's baby" saying it was his idea and design. I thought surely he must have the advice and help of some engineers.

I tried to find the engineers. There weren't any. But I found a few people who thought it might have been better if Allen stayed down in the southwest somewhere on the ranch he went to when the war came along. They thought it seemed advisable for him to turn to agriculture.

There was one thing I could be thankful for—what if I had persevered in trying to make Alaska with the old Alma? It was bad enough having all the troubles I had with it and the light plant on the way back. Perish the thought of having had all those things happen away off in the northern wilderness.

Then I decided to do away with the front passenger seat in the jeep.

I had the tool box underneath it cut out and a large flat gasoline tank built upon which someone could sit uncomfortably in case I carried a passenger. Said passenger would be obliged to sit Buddha fashion.

I examined the plumbing installations. The toilet had a valve away down in back at the floor which was very difficult to reach and which had to be turned and turned and turned about a dozen times to open and then as many times to close. That was the only means of flushing the toilet.

Since there were five receptacles to be drained I wondered just what hook-up they had arranged to facilitate the drainage problem. Of all the shocks I'd had in trailerdom so far I think this was the greatest.

The good looking kitchen sink assembly (two white enamel sinks, chrome swing faucet, spray gadget) was originally intended for a home or apartment and was too heavy to be built in a trailer, but it did make an attractive looking kitchen. The drain pipe was the chrome pipe which came with the unit and was stuck down through the floor with no threads on the end of it and no possible way of connecting a drain hose to it.

The toilet ended underneath the floor with a threaded one-inch pipe to which an adaptor could be added for attaching a 3/4-inch hose. The lavatory in the bathroom went through in a chrome drain pipe with no way for hose connections. And, hard as it may be to believe, the drain for the shower bath was a piece of stove pipe sticking down through the floor.

I walked into Spencer's office and told him since neither he nor any of the rest of them had ever lived in or traveled in a trailer there were a few things they'd better learn. I asked him if he didn't realize that the drains had to be arranged so that they could all be carried off in one hose or go into one sewer connection. Then I described the outlets in my trailer. He called Allen into his office and asked him if it was true they were using stove pipe in the shower. Allen said yes and admitted there was no way of hooking a hose connection. He thought a clay soil pipe might be attached somehow.

In a burst of anger Spencer said, "Call up the goddamn factory and stop production." Then with anger mounting he whirled at me with, "No wonder your trailer won't heat. Beany has ruined it. He's cut holes through the floor big enough to stick your elbow through and spoiled our whole heated floor system. Goddamn the whole thing! We should never have taken on a special job—I hate them—I should have known better —they're a goddamn nuisance—never again!" And he started throwing things around his desk.

I had heard of his tantrums. So here was one and I didn't know whether to start yelling back at him or walk out. I walked meekly out thinking I'd better save my tantrum for when he was calm and more apt to hear what I had to say.

The trailer should have been designed with all the drain pipes coming together INSIDE the trailer with one convenient outlet underneath to which a hose could be connected. Even in the trailer parks with a sewer connection for each trailer, they are fixed for a drain hose to go into the sewer. Unless parked permanently, a trailer would certainly not be equipped with a clay soil pipe arrangement. With the toilet-garbage disposal, which is the ideal thing for a trailer, all the waste is so thoroughly ground and mixed with water that it flushes out very easily through a garden hose.

I went to see what Beany was doing and asked him why they did not build a practical plumbing arrangement. "Oh those guys don't use trailers - they just make'em." Beany had worked for them before their Syracuse factory burned. He didn't like trailers. He didn't like Spencer.

It was when he drew the new trailer to a gas station to fill the system with water that I learned nothing Beany did would work. All the pipes and valves were hooked up wrong, AND EVERY SINGLE CONNECTION IN THE ENTIRE PLUMBING SYSTEM LEAKED. The entire trailer was flooded in three minutes!

Back to the factory it went. Beany blamed the guys who installed the plumbing fixtures. They blamed him. Noble blamed Disher for not hustling the work along to completion. Disher blamed Noble. And so it went. Beany said, "You'll be pickin' up dirt, sand, or mud in water as you go along. That will finally stop up the leaks."

I found out later that he had actually pumped a lot of mud into the system to try to stop the leaks that way. When he installed a quarter turn valve on the pipe leading to the toilet where it could be conveniently reached, it leaked a regular fountain of water. Beany's remark, when I called his attention to that was, "Well, you've got the other valve at the floor and if you turn that off it will stop the other from leaking."

In the first place any moron would know I had the second one put in to avoid using the first. And the first, original valve was NOT between the water source and the other valve - it was BEYOND the leaking valve. Did Beany know beans? Did Beany know ANYTHING?

When the pump didn't work no matter what pipes you opened or closed, Beany said, "You'll just have to carry a large tub of water on the trailer floor just inside the front door. That'll be easy to shovel snow into up there in the north country. And you can keep a hose across the floor from the pump into the tub." Then it dawned on me fully that Beany knew nothing.

Sometimes women have a heck of a time getting along with men because male pride is hurt if a woman shows more intelligence about anything in the mechanical line. I guess Beany was that way. When he found I wasn't just a sissy he could flirt with he had no use for me whatsoever. He called me "Klondike Pete" and whenever he saw me coming he'd say, "Here comes my FAVORITE girl friend."

When Beany began to suggest that I owed him and his carpenter a

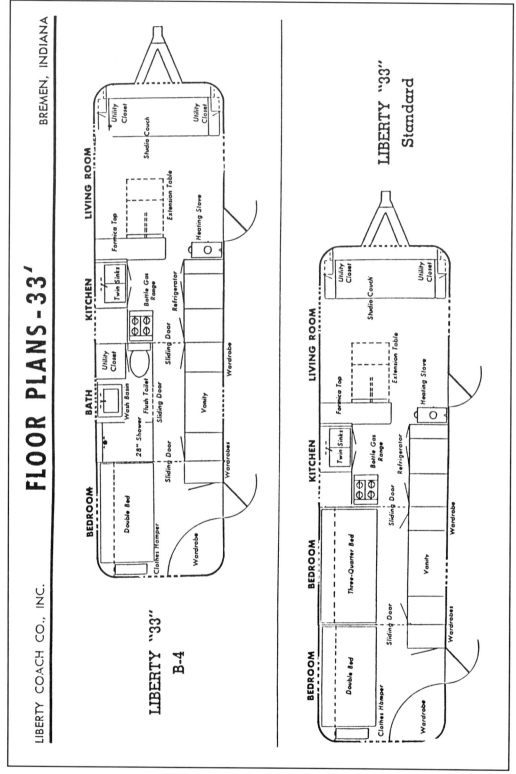

FLOOR PLANS - 33'

LIBERTY COACH CO., INC.   BREMEN, INDIANA

LIBERTY "33"
B-4

LIVING ROOM

Utility Closet

Studio Couch

Utility Closet

Formica Top

Extension Table

Heating Stove

KITCHEN

Twin Sinks

Bottle Gas Range

Refrigerator

Sliding Door

Wardrobe

BATH

Utility Closet

Wash Basin

Flush Toilet

28" Shower

Sliding Door

Sliding Door

Vanity

Wardrobes

BEDROOM

Double Bed

Clothes Hamper

Sliding Door

Wardrobe

Wardrobe

LIBERTY "33"
Standard

LIVING ROOM

Utility Closet

Studio Couch

Utility Closet

Formica Top

Extension Table

Heating Stove

KITCHEN

Twin Sinks

Bottle Gas Range

Refrigerator

Sliding Door

Wardrobe

BEDROOM

Three-Quarter Bed

Sliding Door

Vanity

Wardrobes

BEDROOM

Double Bed

Clothes Hamper

Wardrobe

considerable amount of money, I said, "I didn't order you to do this job. You are working for the Spencers. You'll have to collect from them and you'll have to pay your carpenter. I didn't tell you to get him and the Spencers wanted to do the cabinet work in their own factory." Then I told him that if he and the Spencers did not get together and finish things up so that I could be on my way within three days I'd go without it.

When I returned to the hotel for my mail and evening meal, Ruth Leman greeted me with, "I wondered if you'll EVER get your trailer now. THE FACTORY HAS CLOSED DOWN." Then she went on with, "And is Mr. Spencer in a mood!"

There were disgruntled men hanging around - laid off with no warning. Some thought it might open up again in a week. No one seemed to know why it had shut down, but there were acres and acres of trailers lined up in the yard which didn't seem to be moving.

Speedy production was emphasized in their business. The more trailers the men could run off the assembly line the more they earned. It is a wonder they were thrown together as well as they were. If one man didn't get a nail in the right place the next guy didn't want to wait for him to change it. If an electric wire was cut too short it was yanked through and fastened in the socket anyway as quickly as possible so as not to cause any delay in the line. When having lunch with Spencer one day he said to me, "Just wait and see how much finer trailers we'll be building when you get back next year."

"If you know how to make them better why aren't you doing it now?" "Oh, that would mean we'd have to stop production for quite a while in order to change all our dies and patterns."

After the assembly line stopped work the repair crew continued to work and the so-called plumbers were around to help Beany. For three days they all worked at trying to stop leaks. Then they drew my old trailer into the factory alongside of the new one to change over my dolly and Murat hitch.

The next day was Sunday with no one around so I moved all my possessions from the old trailer into the new one. It took me from 8 a.m. till 3 a.m. (next morning) to get moved. Then, before going to bed in the new trailer I cleaned the old one thoroughly and polished all the woodwork.

After three hours sleep the factory noises woke me up. I got up to find the oil stove leaking all over the floor. Most of the day was spent taking it apart and soldering the oil tank. They lost a nut off the top of the carburetor. Said I didn't need it. I found out later I needed it very much. I went in to settle up with Spencer. He began to do some figuring. The figures grew into something much higher than I had expected. I had the notes of the figures Mac had given me—the factory price of the new trailer, the figure Mac quoted him as saying he would allow for the old trailer, and I decided the bunk beds, the gas stove and butane which I was leaving out would pay for Beany's installations. When I mentioned the agreement he had made with McKenney which had brought me to Bremen to get one of his trailers he flew into a tantrum which made the other tantrums I had seen look like a dish of jello.

He denied ever making any such arrangements with Mac. I said I would get Mac on the phone immediately and let him talk with him. He wouldn't let me. So I sat there while he ranted and raved and paced the floor and tore up bills and papers till he finally said, "Well, give me your check then for what you think you owe and go out and get your bill of sale."

Then Earl McManus and Chuck Gardner threw all their ability and time and energy into helping me. They proved to be as good plumbers as they were electricians. They immediately understood every phase of my water system and all the various functions the pump could and should perform for me.

My new trailer gets a roof. Of course it all had to come out and work to be done over again and the fittings had to be tightened or fixed to stop the leaks, the spray gadget

in the kitchen changed, the proper kind of flushing valve installed on the toilet, and a valve put on top of the water tank so it could be used either as a storage tank or a pressure tank. We put my oxygen egg back in to increase the pressure capacity of the pump when using the big tank as the storage supply. Beany had discarded the egg and I had a devil of a time finding it.

It was wonderful after all those many miserable weeks around the factories to have the fun of watching a couple of intelligent fellows catch on instantly to what I wanted and doing an expert job of everything they undertook. I had a hilarious good time while the boys thoroughly enjoyed their work and stuck to it day and night to get me rolling on my way as soon as possible.

Both the boy's families invited me to some fine dinners in their homes, and I fell in love with a pretty little long haired tabby kitten whose job it was to keep the mice out of the Gardner Electric Shop. I fell so hard for her that Chuck presented her to me for a mascot and companion. When the newspaper got wind of it all they took pictures of the presentation of the kitten and did a big story about my proposed adventure. I named her Sweetie.

When I pulled out the boys gave me about fifty post cards addressed to them for me mail along the way.

Sweetie enjoyed roaming around the inside of my trailer the entire trip.

13. GETTING RELIGION IN HAVRE

(Iris headed back for Montana where the weather was deteriorating rapidly. She noted 20-foot drifts along the road in some places and had her share of mechanical problems including a frozen radiator, flat tires, and trouble with the trailer hitch and springs. She noted that nevertheless all the local town newspapers commented on the huge trailer being a "palace" and very comfortable.)

After the wind and dust subsided the next morning, I struck out for Havre, covering the 43 miles easily in an hour and a quarter.

And that was like getting back home! What a welcome! When I pulled up in front of Odden Motors people started rushing over from all directions—they were so excited about my new trailer. Rose came running over to give me a big hug and then hustled back to put the tea kettle on.

Rose and Jim were still holding forth at the gas station. But I preferred parking in a nice spot Odden had cleared for me back of his garage where he said I could have all the juice I wanted (without swiping it from the power company) and also hook up with running water.

It was a sunny, pleasant spot, all open to the south, and a most convenient location. I was delighted since I knew I'd be in Havre until something could be done about changing my jeep motor. I also knew that by the time I got that done it would be unwise to attempt the northern roads until after the spring thaws were over.

The terribly long wait for the trailer in Indiana had spoiled my chance of getting over the winter road to Alaska and I was bitterly disappointed about missing it. Everyone I had talked with who knew much about the road said it was at its very best in mid-winter. But that was that and here I was.

If my financial problems had not been growing serious I would have had no thought except the pleasure of being able to hang around and absorb a lot more of this interesting part of Montana. I knew now that if I did not like Alaska well enough to stay up there and work for awhile I'd have to mortgage my farm to get back home. But I knew worry wouldn't help and that I'd get along somehow. I was GOING to see

Alaska and the country in between, and I was DETERMINED to push through this experiment in trailer travel and living and PROVE that it COULD be done the way I thought it SHOULD be done.

There was no giving up or turning back. It was a tough assignment I had given myself. If some big company had only been backing me in this. I had been sent on trips by large wealthy industrial concerns where I hadn't a worry in the world. Now—to have undertaken this on my own—well, only a millionaire should have done it.

What surprised me the most in Montana was finding a large number of religious fanatics. If an intelligent person would like to make a little study of what harm the church is capable of doing, Havre, Montana would provide some nice examples and good case histories.

I don't see how people could live in that grand state without being big and broad-minded. A Pentecostal group showed me what a menace to society certain narrow religious faiths can be. Their strict followers think no one should read anything but the bible. It seems to me the bible is something to be read and studied only by very intelligent and highly educated people.

To my amazement there were families who could well afford to give their children the very best in the way of education who would not allow them to go further than the eighth grade. Had it not been for the truant officer they would have deprived their children of even that much education. Children who had a real yen for learning and reading were not allowed a glance into any popular periodicals or books. All movies were taboo, even the few very fine pictures of real educational value and high artistic quality—nothing was "good" enough.

At home they offered their children such drab monotony it was no wonder many of them strayed from the fold.

I watched one such family at close range. Mr. Sutton had done enormously well with his ranching venture. As his income increased and he was well able to build a nice modern home for his family, his wife (the most religious member of the family) objected. Such material things did not interest her. She did not wish to see the others in the family devoting time and attention to any more elaborate manner of living than that which they were maintaining in their three-room shack located in a very unattractive little hollow out on the prairie far from any water supply. Mr. Sutton frequently tried to persuade her of the advantages of a pretty house with running water in an attractive setting near the spring. She couldn't see it. Their homestead shack had been good enough for their first years and could continue to be good enough.

In acquiring the last tract of land to add to his large ranch Mr. Sutton had also acquired a very good house. He thought and hoped the little wife would be interested enough to take advantage of this home already built and standing there vacant. When I looked through that house with the fourteen-year-old daughter, Dorothy, she stood in the window of one of the bedrooms upstairs for a long time thoughtfully gazing out over the flowering shrubs in the yard and beyond to the horizon over Wildhorse Lake. With a sigh I heard her say, half to herself, "Oh wouldn't it be wonderful to have a real room all my own with such a beautiful view from my very own window?"

If the older sister could have lived in a home where she could have been proud to bring her friends, she might not have found the home and the attentions of a married man in town so attractive. Mrs. Sutton told people she was accompanying Edith to a beauty culture school in another Montana city but everyone knew it was to have a baby and leave it there for adoption. Upon their return Mrs. Sutton used to speak proudly of the nice figures of her other daughters, adding, "it seems strange that Edith's figure was never so good—she always did have a large stomach."

Poor Edith found life more tolerable away from the old home town.

I did not foresee Dorothy's following the example of Edith, but instead to become a nervous, neurotic old maid. Then there was another young girl who showed all the signs of becoming a little terror sure to stray from the fold with even greater vengeance than the older one.

There was so much hypocrisy in the mother's fanatical religious devotion. When I attended her church and heard the preacher tell the congregation very emphatically that it did not matter how many good deeds they did, those deeds were absolutely worthless, bad, of no value unless they had the FEAR of God in their hearts. The men and women sat there so filled with devout emotion that their eyes became full of tears and frequently brimmed over and poured down their cheeks.

Then since it didn't matter what they did while they had this fear of God, Mr. Olson went home and opened up a dam which flooded a large parcel of land his neighbor, Mr. Sutton, had recently acquired. Olson resented the fact that Sutton had done so well with ranching that he could buy the land before Olson could acquire it. It was sure to produce a fine crop of hay each year, a tremendous help to any rancher fortunate enough to own it. The dam had been there for a great many years and had never been opened. There was no reason whatsoever that it should be opened, no reason except that it would give Olson the satisfaction of sitting back to watch his neighbor suffer the loss of that valuable crop of hay.

And Mrs. Sutton, at home, seemed to think there was nothing wrong in unmercifully nagging her husband from morning to night, talking about him behind his back in front of the children in such a way that when Dorothy saw her father coming toward the house she said, "Oh hush mummy, here comes daddy."

Rather than stay home and keep house for her husband (who had to remain on the ranch) Mrs. Sutton would spend the winters in town to be nearer her church and all its activities. A nightly bible class occupied every evening and while busy with these highly spiritual activities the two little girls were left alone to take care of themselves, sometimes falling in with some very undesirable companions.

Dorothy would sometimes come home from school crying. The youngsters from families not of her faith would make fun of her strange ideas and the strict rules of behavior imposed upon her by her mother. They had a radio but it was turned on only for the church broadcasts.

They looked upon dancing as a horribly evil thing. According to Mr. Sutton it could lead only to rough and tough liquor joints where girls were led astray.

These religious groups are sending missionaries all over the world to convert the so-called pagan who adheres to the native religion of remote places "not yet Christian" (as Mr. Webster defines pagan). I hope they do not succeed in "converting" many of them. Some of the pagan religions have much more that is fine than these narrow minded, ignorant, bigoted missionaries could every bring them. The missionaries would be shocked if you were to suggest that they might be much better human beings if they themselves could be converted and taught to follow the teachings of Buddha and Confucius. Would Mrs. Sutton or Mr. Olson be what they are if they were followers of the Cardinal Virtues of Confucianism which are listed as: "filial piety, benevolence, justice, propriety, intelligence, fidelity?" Or if they followed in the "Eightfold Path" which a disciple of Buddha lists as: "right belief, right resolve, right word, right act, right life, right effort, right thinking, right meditation."

I think it would be shocking if we knew how many people followed a religion doing more harm than good, blocking the education, progress, health and well-being of a great a portion of our population. The followers of such cults, creeds and faiths are sick, both mentally and physically, and there are such great numbers of them - something ought to be done about it.

These people cannot go along with our civilization any more than the members of the Amish church in Indiana can drive along Route 6 in their little old black buggies with no windows through which they can watch traffic to the side or rear. They drive right down the road thinking the Lord will protect them - but He doesn't always. They make a turn with no signal to drive off on some little road to the left. The big heavy transcontinental trucks roaring past in both directions know they will sustain very little, if any, damage to themselves if they hit one of these spindly things but they don't like to smear the buggy and its occupants and the horse all over the pavement in some desperate maneuvers to try to avoid hitting it. There are altogether too many disasters in which the truck drivers and also the divinely protected buggy drivers are fatally injured.

14. PECULIAR CUSTOMS

It was a jolly reunion when, on August 27th, Jim and Rose Scriven reached Grande Prairie. After all their plans, preparations and hopes, and their stopover of nearly a year in Havre, they were finally on their way to Alaska. Their truck house was very comfortable and they had a load of camping, hunting and fishing equipment including a fine rubber boat. Their old Pekinese pet's nose was out of joint by their acquisition of an adorable little Chewawa puppy.

As usual, Jim had something to fix and my Kohler electric plant mounted in my jeep came in handy as it did to several others I had met along the way who had no means of using electric tools. I drove up along side the truck house to let Jim plug in his electric drill.

J.A. Whitlock was the very first person I had met who knew how to drive a jeep. The previous owners, dealers, agents, garage men, and soldiers—NONE of them really knew how to drive one.

In fact the driving instructions in the service manual are so wrong that I wrote the factory and told them them they'd better rewrite the page about shifting gears after I learned from Whitlock how it should be done. The service manager of the Willys factory thanked me for the information and said the manual would be changed.

There is only one right way to shift those gears and you'd think the people who manufactured it would know how, but they didn't. Various boys in service who had practically lived in jeeps usually said, "Oh we just crashed 'em in and if they wore out there were always new ones."

Inadequate brakes on the trailer were a constant worry to me and retarded my speed. I didn't dare go as fast as I might have if I could have relied on good brakes. It seemed to me a trailer should be equipped with air brakes like the busses have. At least they should have more powerful brakes installed in such a way that if the trailer should break away from the car, the brakes would automatically be applied. I consulted all the brake experts I could find but none of them could figure out a way to improve mine, at least not without great expense or practically rebuilding the carriage with bigger wheels.

It is so much fun to watch the tourists come and go. Each evening I wonder who's going to roll in. Most are folks on their way to or from Alaska. There isn't a soul just lukewarm in his opinions regarding

Alaska or the Alaska Highway. They either hate it or are wild about it.

One couple in a nice car turned around and came back after going as far as Whitehorse where they had only six hundred miles of good road left to Fairbanks. Another couple spent only four hours in Fairbanks and came back so mad they'll never stop regretting the trip.

My five old jeep tires set the Canadian customs officials in a dither. The Collector of Customs and Excise and his assistants spent hours in Edmonton yesterday working fiendishly hard over the problem.

Had I been willing to surrender them to the Crown everything would have been jolly. But I didn't feel I could afford to make the King of England a present of five old jeep tires which still have some wear left in them. When I suggested paying duty on them so that I could have the privilege of selling them here, the somber faces lightened a bit and that seemed a solution until the first assistant recalled that no United States passenger car tires can be sold in Canada.

Couldn't I store them with a garage keeper in Athabasca until my return from Alaska? No, it just wouldn't be safe having United States passenger car tires lying around anywhere in Canada except in bond in the custody of the National Revenue Office in Edmonton. You'd think they were atom bombs.

Those tires MUST be immediately transported OUT of Canada. Couldn't I possibly take them along with me as far as Snag Harbor? To carry five wheels and tires in or on top of the jeep with all else I have in and on it—impossible. To have them ride inside the trailer—there wouldn't be room left for me and my kitten. To carry them on the roof of the trailer—impossible to fasten them there, and certainly not good for the roof.

To ship them about four thousand miles back home to Vermont would cost too much. To ship them to Alaska—that would be very expensive. Well, yes I suppose I can ship them to a party I know in Montana. But hasn't the Canadian government a little more sympathy for their guests who suffer endless tire troubles because of Canada's atrocious roads?

They want American tourists more than they want anything else in the world. Their greatest hopes lie in the American dollar the tourists spend here. Maybe they are keeping many of their main thoroughfares all but impassable in order to milk more dollars out of the poor travelers in the terrific bills they usually have to pay for repairs, towing, tires, etc.

But all that concerns the gentlemen who occupy these dignified offices in their gray striped suites, spats, and little waxed mustaches is their duty to the Crown and the holiness of the law. They give the orders of their strict and prim procedures with pursed lips that show their years of training in the pronunciation of prunes and prisms.

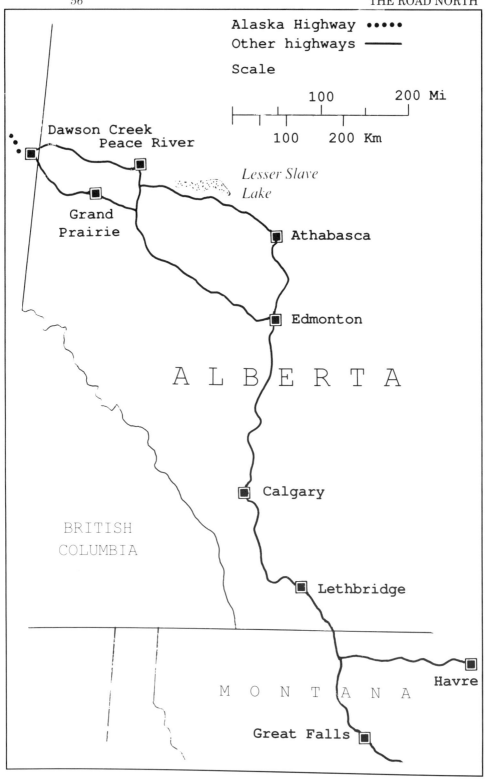

When the first assistant took me to the express office in his highly polished 1935 Ford I told him I thought it was a crime that the people in Canada have to pay so terribly much more for their automobiles and refrigerators than in the states.

The Athabasca Echo.

"We no longer allow the importation of refrigerators," he said.

"You are probably making your own then," I said, "which I think is a very good idea."

"Oh no," he said, "we do not need refrigerators and we do not want our people spending their money on something so foolish and unnecessary. Our economy cannot afford it."

Aghast, I said, "You don't consider refrigerators a great convenience and very helpful toward a better way of living?"

"Not at all," he said, "our people have been getting along perfectly well without refrigerators and they can just as well continue to do so."

When I saw the town, Athabasca, on the map, I hustled through the big crowded city of Edmonton thinking that if I were going to be stuck I'd find it more interesting to be stuck in Athabasca.

And stuck I was. Having to change a tire on the rear of the jeep about every eighty miles got to be too much.

The country around Athabasca began to look and feel something like Vermont with the road winding among densely wooded green hills with occasional clearings for farms.

Athabasca had a familiar ring but it was sometime before I recalled that it was probably Robert Service's poem, "The Man from Athabasca," in which I had first heard that interesting sounding name.

The population is about a thousand. A great many Indians live like gypsies in the outlying sections and farming is carried on by Ukrainians, Poles and Danes. The Indians have mixed with the French and there are a great many "breeds," as the half-breeds are called. The rougher element of Ukrainian laborers and loafers are usually referred to as "Bohunks."

I looked for fresh vegetables in the grocery stores on Main Street and there and none were to be found. A long search finally brought me to a head of lettuce—big and green and strong and tough—like the people, I thought. Finally I discovered some onions—tough and strong and dark, a cross between red and white onions—again like the people. Some horrible looking dirty carrots turned up in one store. To my surprise they were sweet and tender—like some of the people, maybe like the dirty, tough-looking drunk who bumped into me and in a soft polite voice said, "I beg your pardon."

When it came time to move the trailer out of the mud in the bus terminal—it had settled deep in the gumbo—it was a tough job. The little old jeep stood up on its hind wheels. It had the 250-pound weight on the front and two gas cans on each front fender. I decided four gas cans on each fender would be better. Then I found I could fasten a spare tire on the hood.

While sitting inside the trailer, sometimes I was amused to hear the remarks of the passersby.

"Jesus Christ what a long trailer! And look at that little jeep on the front end of it. How in the hell can that little jeep pull it?"

The day after I parked there a couple of boys passed by. "Gee, that's a big son of a gun of a trailer."

"Yeah and the little jeep can travel with that thing. I know. I saw her coming into town yesterday."

A little tot came by with his mother.

"What's the train doing here, mom?"

"That's not a train."

"It is too a train. And oh look mom, the engine's a jeep. Does the engineer ride in the jeep?"

I was ready to pull out on September 5, 1948, a year and five days after leaving Vermont. All the tires on the trailer and jeep had been remounted with the proper flaps. All my mechanical equipment had been carefully checked. J.A. was interested in everything and wanted to make sure it was all in perfect running order. In fact he was so intrigued with the idea of traveling with such a setup it was just about all I could do to keep him from going right along with me.

15. BROADWAY IN CANADA

Finally at Dawson Creek, a huge arrow and signpost marks Mile 0, the beginning of the Alaska Highway. The word Alcan had been used for a time but there was so much objection to the name that it was officially and very definitely dropped. The word can still be found on an occasional restaurant sign, but it is generally considered poor taste. It also appears in magazines or newspapers in the states, being used by reporters who evidently dashed up and down so fast they did not learn how taboo it has become.

Dawson Creek must have been a busy town during the construction of the highway. There, at the end of the Northern Alberta Railways, a railhead camp was established for the thousands of engineer troops who arrived in March 1942 to smash through a back door to Alaska. Ten thousand soldiers and six thousand civilians accomplished the mighty and almost incredible achievement with unprecedented speed and completed the 1,600 miles of road with its 200 bridges in less than eight months. To build eight miles of road a day, beautifully engineered with 24 feet between shoulders, and to build it over mountains, through forests never before penetrated, over hundreds of miles of muskeg (which is passable in winter when frozen but turns to a soggy muck 10 to 20 feet deep in summer), was an accomplishment to say the least— this "Burma Road" of America.

The work was a race against time and a terrific gamble with Old Man Weather. The trail which led north from Dawson Creek crossed the Peace River on the ice in winter and by ferry in summer. In spring when the river was thawing and the ice moving out, or in fall when it was freezing, it could not be crossed. The ice usually went out in April.

They rushed to get all the equipment possible across the river before the ice went out. The break-up usually lasted several weeks and would have meant serious delay—with the Japanese in the Aleutians.

Fort St. John, a small settlement twenty miles beyond, became a base camp. From there, 250 miles of bumpy winter road wound its way through wild, desolate country to Fort Nelson. The command wanted to start building the highway north and south from Fort Nelson, north and south from Whitehorse, and south from Alaska.

To quote from a little booklet dedicated by the Canadians to the men who built the Alaska highway, edited by Don Menzies:

"The race to Fort Nelson started.

"Drivers wheeling multiple-tired trucks began to shuttle back and forth over the bumpy 250 miles. Farmers' trucks and cartage companies were pressed into service. It was a race against the thaw - a tough, tiring race that taxed the stamina of the strongest. The men worked long shifts. Motors were seldom turned off. Drivers relieved one another but the trucks continued the long grind. Some men worked day and night; some for 60 hours at a stretch. Grades were steep, a few at 45-degree angles. Coming down these grades with several tons of equipment loaded behind proved to be tricky and hazardous.

"The days became brighter and the thaw started, but they kept on, floundering in a sea of mud, shoving and winching their way north.

"River ice began to heave. The engineers laid down sawdust and planks to prevent thawing where trucks crossed the rivers.

"Just as rivers looked as though they were going to break up and muskeg become impassable, General Frost came along one night and froze the whole route tighter than an iceberg. Ice cracks in rivers were cemented, the soggy muskeg froze stiff, and everyone danced with glee. It gave the soldiers an extra week to get their supplies north to Fort Nelson. Hundreds of trucks were used day and night.

"A pilot who flew along the route one night said, 'That stretch to Fort Nelson looked like Broadway. It seemed to be lit up all the way with the headlights of the trucks.'

"Finally the rivers started to go out but the engineers had won the first round."

Similar advance parties went into Whitehorse, Yukon, through Skagway via the White Pass and Yukon Railway. A colored unit went in through Alaska and started work near the Yukon-Alaskan border. I often wondered how those fellows from the south ever stood the cold up there. Yet the entire construction took place during the warmest part of the year.

Some of the boys might have preferred the extreme cold of mid-winter to the mosquitoes. I was fortunate in missing the mosquitoes, but ran into many a tale about the "dive-bombers" as they were usually called. There were the two soldiers who pumped a couple of hundred gallons of gasoline into one before they realized it wasn't a Douglas transport. And there were the two small mosquitoes who were feasting on a couple of boys inside a tent when one mosquito said to the other, "Let's take 'em outside to finish 'em." "Naw," said the first, "If we do the big fellers'll get 'em."

Bears were interested spectators during the construction of the road but the boys must have done a good deal of shooting because very few

I often wondered
how those fellows
from the south
stood the cold up
there.

There was no
shortage of trees
to make a cordu-
roy road across
the muskeg.

The engineers laid down sawdust and planks to prevent thawing where trucks crossed the rivers. Often temperatures fell so low that machinery would not operate and skin could be frozen to metal in seconds. Motors were seldom turned off.

Summer rains created a sea of mud and stuck vehicles were a common sight.

Temporary timber trestles or pontoon bridges were used to cross the numerous rivers after the ice melted. More than 200 permanent bridges were eventually constructed.

The 1523-mile
highway officially
opened on
November 20,
1942. A ceremony
took place at
Soldier's Summit
above Kluane Lake.
Representatives
from both Canada
and the United
States partici-
pated.

wild animals are now seen near the highway.

Menzies says, "Even-tempered and philosophical, the Indians couldn't grasp what all the speed was about. They understood that a road was being built, but why, they asked, was everybody in such a hurry? When told about Hitler's plans for world conquest, one of them said, 'What's he want all that land for? He sure die some day.'"

After a good season on his trapline an Indian up on Teslin Lake had bought himself a car. When it finally arrived, shipped by rail and water, George realized that a car needs a road. He cleared out three miles of road through the bush and decided to make the car pay for itself by operating up and down his private road and charging his friends for pleasure rides. He was probably pleased about the highway.

The finest roadbuilding equipment ever assembled was used. Menzies called the bulldozer a land battleship and quotes one "cat" driver as saying, "We just walk'em down, shove'em aside and let'em lay." He was talking about the endless miles of trees. The biggest headaches were where the long stretches of muskeg had to be corduroyed as the equipment and the men wallowed in a sea of slime.

When the road, built and paid for by the U.S., was turned over to Canada, the question of equipment became a serious problem. There was a tremendous amount of valuable machinery which would have been most useful in maintaining the road. There were pieces of road equipment which had never been used, some crates which had not yet been opened, hundreds of boxes of new replacement parts, tools, and electric light plants (some slightly used and some never used). Many storehouses along the highway were packed full.

The U.S. government said it would not pay to transport all that stuff back down into the states. The Canadian government said it could not be left there. It would hurt the business of Canadian manufacturers.

The U.S. would not take it out. Canada would not buy it or accept it as a gift. So the Canadian government had their people dig huge ditches. They smashed what they could before burying it. Then the Canadian army guarded those ditches and no one dared be caught trying to salvage anything.

Now many parts of the highway through Canada are in bad shape and growing rapidly worse. Canada hasn't the men, money or machines to maintain the road. Six men and a few very decrepit pieces of road equipment are struggling to keep up each hundred miles of the road. At the rate things are going they will have no graders or road machinery left in a very short time. The busiest man on the road crews in Canada is the fellow who goes along marking the washouts and bad places with little red flags. I passed some very dangerous spots and it seemed a crime to see such a magnificent feat of engineering neglected in many places.

The shock of learning what happened to all that valuable road equipment and machinery is something I'll never forget.

As I pulled out from Dawson Creek it was good to get onto the big wide, solid roadbed of the highway. Not far below Fort St. John there was a delightful place to pull off and park overnight down by the water's edge under the shadow of the giant towers of the Peace River Bridge. The two-lane suspension bridge 100 feet above the water cost the U.S. government $1,750,000.

One of its 190-foot towers began to lean and in January 1948 it was discovered that the swirling waters of the river had gouged a great hole around the base of the tower. In a desperate effort to save the bridge, divers had to work under the ice in the frigid water. They built a coffer dam to protect it from further undermining until they could reinforce it in the spring. They did not count on record-breaking spring floods. There were anxious weeks while the ice was going out and all the engineers could do was sit on the bank and watch and hope. The betting was 50 - 50. If the dam did not hold, the tower would go and the bridge would be washed downstream like a huge cob web. It held.

16. "YOU'LL NEVER MAKE IT."

Fort St. John appealed to me. It seemed a good little town, and very friendly, but I stopped only long enough to take a quick look up and down its two blocks of Main Street, get my mail and leave a forwarding address.

At Mile 101 the small settlement of Blueberry had recently burned and there was nothing left but a couple of gas pumps which had miraculously escaped the flames. Sitting there in front of the pumps what should I see but The Rover. That was the name printed high on the front of the Scrivens' homemade truck house. Jim and Rose were headed BACK.

"The Indians can have it, " said Jim. "We've had enough of it. If we ever go to Alaska it will be by boat. There's nothing more to see along the highway. It's all just like this only the hills get worse. You'll NEVER make it with your outfit."

They had turned back at Mile 201 after having a lot of trouble with their truck. That truck of theirs was assembled with too much variety of parts. No one should undertake this trip without orthodox equipment.

But think of all the time and preparation Jim and Rose had put into their plans! And when they had stopped over in Grande Prairie they were still boasting about how they had the best outfit on the road.

I was ready to look for a night's parking when I reached Mile 143 and saw a cabin resort being constructed on an old army barracks site. Since they had a service station of sorts I thought I'd have my jeep greased, but I should have heeded Sandy Singer's admonition to keep out of old campgrounds. He had told me I would find them tempting places to park but that they were strewn with so many nails that I'd probably pick up at least one. I did. The man who greased the jeep changed the trailer tire but had no way of repairing the flat.

I had crossed off my list some of the gas stations or stop-overs various tourists had told me to avoid. Trutch, Mile 201, was one of them. I stopped for gas anyway. I sized up the man as an independent sort who might not bother to be overly pleasant to everyone, but he looked interesting and a bit of conversation made me think he would be worth knowing. He invited me into his office to see some pictures and I spent an extremely interesting evening listening to him and looking at his collection of thrilling photographs of the construction of the highway.

Now, back home, I eagerly look in my weekly *Alaska Highway News* for a column by H. Noakes called "News 'n Nonsense from Trutch" and

Little
Smokey
Inn

will always be grateful for visiting with the author at Mile 201.

Next morning, about 20 miles beyond Trutch, on a sudden, short, steep curve, I stalled for the first time. At least I thought I was stalled. There was one thing I was determined NOT to do and that was to abuse my clutch. So I just set the brakes, got out and blocked the wheels and wondered who would be the first one to come along and whether the stories I had heard were true about how kind and generous people along the highway were about helping each other up hills.

A big bus came along in a few minutes and the driver hopped out with a cheery, "Throw me your chain." He hooked on and we rolled up over the top where we both had a good laugh. I hadn't needed any help at all. I had eased myself up all the way with the chain between us hanging slack. All I really needed was moral support.

But at Mile 252 a bridge curved across Beaver Creek and I really did stall on a very steep hill. Not far behind me came a jeep with UNIVER-SITY OF ALASKA in big letters on the front of it. Out jumped three boys and quick as a wink they unhooked their small luggage trailer, hooked their jeep on to mine and we zoomed up the hill.

That called for a search through the trailer till I came up with some cans of the beer that made my birthplace famous. Since the boys seemed in no hurry I had a delightful time listening to the story of their trip.

They had taken a year's leave from the university and toured the entire length of the Western Hemisphere with their jeep, driving it over every inch of the Inter-American Highway over which it was possible to drive. They had put it on the rails to cover one missing link in Central America and flown it over another. Then, after touring South America they had shipped it by boat from Buenos Aires to New York where they picked it up and were now on their way back for the opening of the fall term. I can't forget the name of one of the boys, George Aiken, same as my old friend and neighbor, the Senator from Vermont.

Seventy-seven miles was not very much to cover in a day, but I did not like to look for parking places after dark. So when I saw convenient looking spots in the late afternoon I usually pulled off for the night.

At Mile 278, Mr. and Mrs. Long were fixing up a tourist camp out of some old barracks. I parked across the road to try to avoid picking up any more nails. When I smelled the odors which came out of Mrs. Long's kitchen I decided to have my evening meal in their attractive, homelike dining room. My appetite was whetted more while watching her prepare food in the immaculate kitchen open to view from the lunch counter. For a dollar I was served a wonderful roast pork dinner with a big fluffy baked potato, fresh crispy crusty homemade bread. A quarter pound of butter was set before each guest.

No wonder it was fast becoming one of the most popular places along the highway. It did not take long for the truck drivers to become aware of the quality of the food and the warm welcome extended by the fine personalities of the Longs.

Conversation that evening centered around the murder which had just taken place nearby. A man who had sold out his business in the states started for Alaska with his thirteen-year-old daughter, advertising for a passenger to ride up with them and share the expenses of the trip. When they got to here the passenger suggested stepping into the woods to shoot a couple of squirrels.

The passenger shot the girl's father, took his roll of $1300, the daughter and the car and drove back to the states, bought a lunch counter, called the girl his sister and set up housekeeping. But he was a member of some sort of gang and shot one of them who started hanging around. When the police questioned him on that he told them he had accidently shot a man up the highway. They escorted him back up to show them, and sure enough. Otherwise no one would ever have known about it.

17. J. A. TO THE RESCUE

On the way to Fort Nelson next morning, my starter gear stuck. I knew of no way to get it working except by rocking back and forth in gear. To rock my eight-ton outfit back and forth was hardly possible so I had to unhook the jeep. As I was doing it a couple of garage men came along and helped me.

The Fort Nelson garage was the first place I came to after picking up the nail at MP143 where I could get the tire fixed. As I pulled up to the garage door the starter stuck again. They showed me how I could get it working by loosening the screws in the case. But they advised me to get a new starter gear.

I phone the Whitlocks in Grande Prairie and they said they could put one on the plane so it would reach me next morning.

Fort Nelson is a tiny settlement, mostly occupied by the families of boys stationed at the big airport nearby.

Some old barracks near the garage were anything but attractive but when a charming girl from Davenport, Illinois, invited me in to tea I was surprised to see how cozy and comfortable she and some of the other young wives had made their apartments.

Weaving up   Bob took me out to see the airport with its lines of jet planes poised
the hills   for take off—a beautiful sight, but an uneasy thought. And so many of
below Trutch. the huge transport trucks traveling up the highway were loaded with jet
planes and parts.

Across the river from the airport lies the original Fort Nelson where a Catholic Mission was established in the wilderness many years ago.

The part for my starter mechanism did not arrive next morning. As it was Sunday I thought I'd better wait over in the hope it would arrive Monday, or possibly be found locked in the mail bag at the Post Office.

It did not come Monday. I didn't want to wait any longer. I got the mechanic to show me again just how to get the gears to mesh in case I got stuck again, left instructions for forwarding the new part if and when it did arrive, and moved along. I couldn't understand why it had not come.

Steamboat Mountain lay ahead. I had been warned many times about it. It sure was a long stiff climb up a series of steep hills. I succeeded in pulling myself up one after another and was just relaxing and thinking I had conquered it when I rounded one of those million curves to find the last and most precipitous grade of all looming up in front of me. I had barely stopped when a big bright orange meat truck came along and pulled me over the top.

It rained that afternoon and I decided that if there were any more steep hills ahead I'd have less chance of making them if they were the least bit slippery. I was following along the Racing River and at Mile 378 I pulled off to the side to park.

Seeing three little white tents off down by the water's edge, I strolled down to investigate. A small crew of government surveyors were stationed there. They had been working up and down the highway all

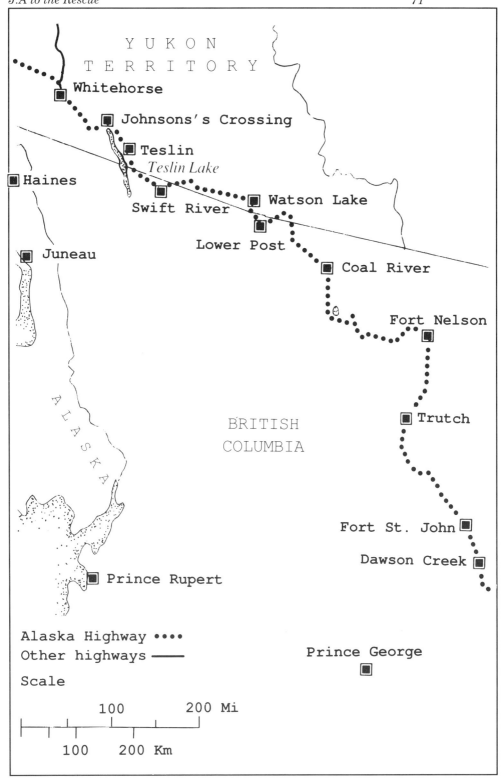

summer surveying all the many plots which had been leased along the roadside for gas stations, cabin courts and lunch rooms. It will not be long before one will find a hamburger or a gas pump around every curve.

It was still raining and I regretted missing a lot of wonderfully scenic picture material. I was in no special hurry to move on, but about 10 o'clock decided to go a few more miles. As I stepped on the starter who should drive up but J.A.

Stories certainly can grow as they roll down the highway. He had been off fishing when I called and talked with his son Saturday about my starter gear. When he returned Monday morning he learned about my having phoned the order and the son had sent it right out on the plane.

Later Monday a trucker went through Grande Prairie with a tale that I was hopelessly stuck with the jeep in pieces at Fort Nelson. J.A. jumped in his car, drove all night, reached Fort Nelson early the next morning, learned that I had gone on but without the starter gear. He went to the airport, met the plane, and sure enough, just as Bob had suspected, the starter gear had been riding back and forth between Grande Prairie and Whitehorse ever since Saturday. He got it and chased on up after me. My starter never again failed me and that new gear isn't in yet.

For many miles through that part of the country the road follows along close to wonderful rivers. Some places I could park so close to the water that I could throw a hose down into it and pump water into the trailer. I didn't take time to do any fishing, but people gave me fish along the way. I didn't like the very large trout very well though they would have been fun to catch. The smaller grayling were better eating.

18. A NEW FRIEND

At Coal River, Mile 533, friendly and talkative Red Kennedy runs the bus station, gas station, meals and lodging house. It was a spacious place and evidently popular as was obvious from the fact that practically all the traffic up and down the highway turned in there. Red was certainly a booster for that part of the country and told of countless things of interest to see and do if one would only stay around long enough to explore places just a little ways back off the road.

Again I was sorry it was dark and rainy because when I followed one of the trails Red suggested I found thrilling rapids and rocks where three rivers come together with a vengeance. With the brilliant yellow popular and dark green pines it would have made some swell Kodachromes. But I couldn't wait around for it to clear up.

I had passed several repeater stations and had been told how they keep the telephone and telegraph communication systems open and in perfect order at all times. They were inviting looking places with huge clean gravel driveways and parking spaces. Seeing gas pumps at one of the first I came to I had turned in only to see a sign saying NO UNAUTHORIZED VEHICLES ALLOWED. I backed myself out as quickly as possible and didn't dare hesitate at any more of them till the evening after leaving Red Kennedy's. It was getting dark and I shouldn't have tried to go further in the rain. Passing the Coal River Repeater Station at Mile 543, I ventured to ask permission to pull off the road for the night. It was very cordially granted.

Next day I went in to thank them. The boys on duty were full of questions about my outfit and especially about my photographic work and equipment. They wanted to see my cameras and darkroom. Then they wanted me to meet their wives and took me around to their various attractive little houses—as usual the drab old barracks were surprising inside, some of them almost elegant.

I was preparing to drive on, but NO— positively no, they must all get together for the evening and have a party and show me some of their slides. It was fun. They were a swell bunch of kids.

Before dark they took me with them to a trapper's cabin. He had gone away for a few days leaving them with the responsibility of feeding his dogs.

A trapper who wants the best possible sled dogs will often keep a wolf for breeding purposes. The wolf, even when caught when very young, can never be tamed. It remains wild and vicious. It is strange that the half breed pups never inherit any of the ugliness but are so very shy, timid, nervous and supersensitive, they can never be trained to be good work dogs. But from these half breeds they can raise pups which have all the qualities they need to make the best possible sled dogs.

Gordon and Margaret Haliburton at the repeater station had a dog they called Foxie. She was half wolf, quarter border collie and quarter McKenzie husky, a beautiful thing and a lovely pet. They had bred her with a full blooded Siberian husky. The result was two magnificent pups. I picked up one of the most irresistible round balls of the softest, silkiest, thickest fluff I ever got my hands on. When I put it down, it started tagging me around. "You've got yourself a dog, Iris," said Gordon.

"Don't tell me you'd give it away—and even if you would I couldn't possibly have a dog. My trailer is completey occupied with a cat," I said.

"You've got yourself a dog, Iris," said Gordon Haliburton. I named her Peater after the repeater station.

"Oh, the pup wouldn't need to live in the trailer. It's an outdoor dog and should never be inside. It could ride with you in the jeep and sleep under the trailer when you're parked till it gets big enough to jump up and sleep on the top of the jeep," said Gordon.

"Don't tempt me. I CAN'T HAVE A DOG. It's too young to take away from its mama anyway."

"It's learning how to eat. I'll show you how to feed it and will give you some of the dog food we use. If you get tired of it or find it too much bother there are a lot of people further north who would give an awful lot to have a dog like that. You'd have no trouble finding a good home for it. We really have more good dogs than we need around here."

So the pup went with me. I named her Peater after the repeater station. And what fun it was having that cuddly lovable thing riding alongside me in the jeep.

It was afternoon when I left the Coal River Station and not far beyond I stalled on a hill. A truck with several fellows on their way to Whitehorse came along and helped me up and then insisted upon staying behind me all the rest of the afternoon in case I needed help again. One of them ran a service station in Whitehorse and was carrying a big drum of gas out of which he sold me enough to fill all my cans and tank at the Whitehorse price which was considerably lower than at the stations along the road.

They had me stop at Allen's Lockout where we got a grand view and took some pictures.

There was a deserted camp at Mile 595 where they said there was a big smooth parking space and they didn't think I'd pick up any nails. They stayed for dinner.

I tipped a pasteboard carton on its side under the trailer as a shelter for little Peater and put a warm wool blanket in it. It poured rain that night and in the morning Peater and blanket and all were in six inches of water.

It poured all the next day and I covered only a hundred miles. At Lower Post I stopped for gas, had a hard time finding anyone interested enough to check my transmission, paid a high price for a horrible lunch and left with a bad impression of Lower Post.

I found a gravel pit in which to park for the night. Gravel pits made ideal parking places. Some of the best had signs saying "Canadian Army Property—Keep Out" but I was beginning to look upon such signs as more of a welcome than otherwise.

Getting an early morning start proved to tough. The rains had caused rock slides and the road crews hadn't cleared them away. Only luck saved me going around a curve at a fairly good speed on a slight down grade. The huge rocks just happened to be lying on the road in such a pattern as to give me barely enough room to slide around past them without going over the bank. That would have given me a good tumble for several hundred feet into the valley below.

That was one of the few early morning starts I had made on the highway—and never again. Even with good brakes on the trailer—which I did NOT have—had those rocks been a few inches either one way or the other I wouldn't be telling this story.

At Rancheria a very nice resort has been fixed up. I pulled in for gas and as the man was filling the tank I heard a hiss which meant a tire was going down. The man who ran the place had gone off for the day and the old gentleman, a school teacher, left in charge, did NOT like to fix flats. "I refuse to own a car just on that account," said he. "Maybe if I just put some air in it you can go on."

In the time it took him to say that much the tire was flat as a pancake. "Go on?!!" said I. "Why the very idea of suggesting such a thing."

"Well, I tell you I DON'T LIKE TIRES."

"This place has been highly recommended to me. You advertise a garage with tire repairing and service of all kinds. I think you'd darn well better have someone here who DOES LIKE TIRES."

With grunts and groans he started fumbling around with some tools in an attempt to take the wheel off the jeep. I couldn't stand watching his clumsy efforts so I got out my overalls and went at it myself. Just as I was removing the wheel, what should I see out of the corner of my eye

but a trailer tire going flat. The school teacher nearly fainted. Fortunately for me, a truck drove in just then to gas up and the old gentleman
enlisted the aid of the driver who said he knew all about patching tires.

Both flats were caused by sharp pieces of gravel getting stuck in the
tire tread and working in. By the time they had cut through into the tube
they made ugly breaks in the tires so I had to have boots put on them.

Almost everyone who tried to drive that road with ordinary tread
tires met with the same difficulty. The kind with small grooves running
round the tire like mine was the very worst type. Heavy treads like the
army or tractor tires, or the knobby snow and mud grips were the best.
I wish I had found that out sooner, but I had to persevere with what I had.
Having bought eleven new tires and twenty-three new inner tubes since
I started, I couldn't very well switch to a different kind now.

19. "BIG DOG EAT LITTLE DOG."

Morley River, Mile 777, was a place not highly recommended, but it
was in a very attractive setting among the pines at a bend in the river.
I was ready to pull off for the night so I thought I would try it out.

I couldn't help but feel the Kimberlins had just stepped out of
Greenwich Village. Their lunch room and lounge had much the same
atmosphere you would expect to find on Eighth Street or Christopher.
They advertised gas and had none. They advertised fresh milk and had
none. I decided this was the reason they had been blacklisted by some
of the tourists. But then I found out the real reason they did not have all
the supplies they wanted and needed.

They were independent and not agents of The British Yukon Navi-
gation Company. The B.Y.N. was one of the most disgusting monopolies
I ever saw. It ran the bus, transportation and gas stations all along the
highway. There were very few who could hold out in business against
them. The Kimberlins were at their mercy for deliveries of gas, oil and
supplies. The B.Y.N. just ignored them half the time, neglecting to make
deliveries.

Kimberlin was negotiating a deal with a trucker who was making
runs to deliver goods in Alaska and figured he would be able to bring
some gas back down on his return trips. By doing so Kimberlin would be
able to undersell the B.Y.N. stations by 14 cents a gallon and still make
his legitimate profit of 8 cents.

A long bridge across the lower end of Teslin Lake led to the village of Teslin. It had a nice store and a modern lodge down on the shore of the lovely lake. I was glad I at least put on a clean, well—pressed pair of slacks to go into the lodge dining room for dinner. It was such a swank little place. The inn, trading post and store all were owned and operated by a retired Mountie who had lived there with his family for 25 years. His daughters helping around the place had been away to school and looked like movie stars.

There was a Catholic Mission and long rows of Indian dwellings. One of the young Indian boys was so intrigued by the trailer he kept following me around while I was parking. I knew how it would thrill him to see the inside so I showed him through. He thought Peater was just about the nicest pup he had ever seen.

Next morning Peater was gone! I hunted and hunted. I walked up and down all the roads through the Indian village. They had a lot of dogs all over the place, terrible looking creatures, most of them apparently half starved. The Indians all looked glum. I asked several of them if they had seen my pup. I always got the same answer—a grunt and, "Sometime big dog eat little dog." Then I would say, "No, I'm sure no big dog has eaten my little dog."

After hunting all morning I learned that there was one of the Royal Canadian Mounted Police stationed there. I looked him up, a nice big Scotchman named Shaw, and told him I was NOT going without my pup. He spent a couple of hours walking all over the Indian settlement with me and told me that in that country it was a terribly serious offense to steal or to harm a dog.

When I told him how young Peater was he said he thought she had wandered off and got lost. I told him she never had and I was sure she never would leave the trailer, jeep or me. The hours went by and I continued to let everyone in the settlement know I was NOT going to drive off without my dog.

Finally when standing in the center of the village talking with the Mountie, a little Indian boy came over to me and said, "I see brown puppy, so big, white feet. I show you." He led me to a deserted shack with a dirt floor, no door, an empty saucer on the floor and poor little Peater crying and trying desperately hard to climb out over a pile of packing boxes which barricaded the doorway.

Shaw still didn't seem to think Indians would steal a dog because of the long prison sentence it would involve if caught. He gave me a chain and told me I ought not to let her run. I never used the chain and Peater never did run away. No one can ever make me believe she barricaded herself in that old Indian shack all on her own. She was such an adorable, lovable, irresistible baby, everyone who saw her wanted her. Many of the travelers I met along the road begged me for her, and she sure had her picture taken lots of times, movies and all.

Beyond Teslin the road was the worst washboard I had yet encountered, but the scenery along the lake was lovely. One of the prettiest bridges was at Johnson's Crossing.

I reached Marsh Lake about six-thirty. Mike Nolan, a retired Mountie, has built a most attractive camp there called Dunrovin. I certainly am glad Sandy Singer had told me they were especially awaiting my arrival there. She had explained that it was a very beautiful place back off the road by the shore of the lake.

Having been told all that I whirled off the road without hesitation on what looked liked a narrow, muddy, treacherous trail leading nowhere. But I knew I could rely upon Sandy's word and sure enough the driveway led into the most delightful spot I had yet seen in the north country, especially with the sun setting magnificently over the lavender snow-covered peaks on the opposite shore, casting purple, gold and rose reflections in the silvery smooth mirror of Marsh Lake.

Mike happened to be away for a few days and I was sorry not to meet him. His eye for beauty was evident in everything about the place, and he no doubt appreciated the picturesque grandeur of that magnificent country in all the seasons of the year.

I spent that evening dancing and talking with a couple of big game hunters from Denver who were waiting for Mike to return and guide them on an expedition. I don't think they enjoyed some of my talk when we became involved in discussing monopolies. You probably need a monopoly or two if you're going to follow the big game hunting seasons around the world. Two weeks at $3000 up here was just a cheap little jaunt for them.

Mike had a beautiful team of five big huskies and little Peater had the time of her life playing with them. "Big dog sometime eat little dog" — my eye! All the big dogs I had seen had been good to Peater. They'd let her grab an ear or tail and hang on for dear life. In all their rough and tumble they never hurt her.

I heard a goodly supply of bear stories, the best of which were told by Dorothy, the bright and charming half Indian girl who was cooking and playing hostess in Mrs. Nolan's absence. She fell in love with Sweetie when she came into the trailer. Though Peater attracted much attention, Sweetie didn't go unnoticed either and usually could be seen sitting at a window and pushing the slats of the Venetian blinds down so she could watch everything that was going on outside. Sweetie did not like cold nor did she like Peater, so I did not need to worry about the possibility of her slipping out when the door was open.

The last ten miles of road to Whitehorse were worse than any I had encountered as far as maintenance was concerned on the highway proper.

It was a ghastly stretch of washboard, holes, loose gravel and soft dirt through which I could hardly pull the trailer on the level. I could see why some tourists had become discouraged at this point and turned back at Whitehorse. Sandy had warned me about this stretch but said conditions improved again north of town and that the best surface of the whole highway would be found after crossing the Alaskan border.

A terrible long steep winding hill led down into Whitehorse.

In the famous old gold rush of '98 Whitehorse was a booming town with the throngs of fortune seekers changing from the Skagway Railroad to the boats which carried them to Dawson City on the Yukon River. The old boats lined upon the river bank are an interesting sight. What stories they could tell! Some of them were used as storage houses and supply depots during the construction of the highway.

Up around the Klondike the map shows Bonanza, Nogold Creek, Silver Hill, Horseshoe Hill, Potato Hill, Starvation Mountain, Mt. Deception, Mt. Fairplay and the towns of Hunker, Chicken and Wounded Moose. And of course there's a Paris.

Old riverboats in Whitehorse were used as storehouses during the highway construction.

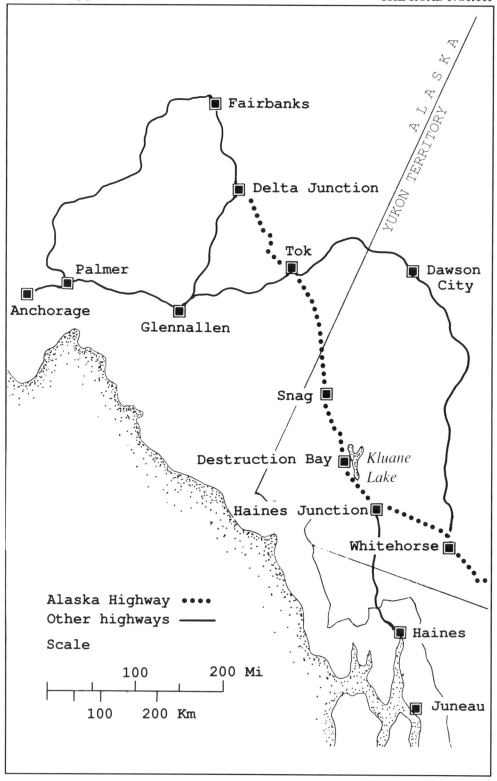

20. "YOU MADE 10 MILES TODAY."

In Whitehorse I found an auto camp. It had electricity, but the current was weak. There was good water and a hose for easy filling. There were nice shops in Whitehorse and I stocked up on fresh groceries and frozen vegetables. But no milk. I hate canned milk. Bought a large can of Klim, powdered milk, which I found I could use hot. I decided next time I met a cow I'd drink her dry.

It took all the jeep had in it to climb the hill out of Whitehorse but I made it. It didn't take long to drive the 80 miles to Canyon Creek on Saturday afternoon. There's no weekend traffic on the highway — it's the same every day of the week.

Just beyond Haines Junction I visited the Agricultural Experiment Station. It was a small affair. Mr. Abbott told me there was very little land that far north which could be used for cultivation — just a small valley there at Mile 1020 which happened to be the right elevation, 2100 feet, where there was a silt loam of 18 to 24 inches over the surface.

Shortly after leaving the farm I met a trailer coming down the road which had a familiar look. It was Mr. Olmstead and the Westcraft. He wanted to get the trailer down from the north before snow and ice. Mrs. Armstrong, who was remaining in Alaska a little longer, was planning to fly down to join him in the states. He warned me of snow ahead. He said that for the first time since hauling the Westcraft, his Cadillac had failed to make a hill that morning and he had to be pulled.

He thought I'd reach Burwash on good dry road, but I was slowed by the miles and miles of gradual climb. A 1000-foot rise in elevation meant a pull for my little jeep and its eight tons behind. And most of the road was so rough I kept anchoring down more and more pieces of furniture in the trailer. Every time I'd go in I'd find something else skidded around to a new position. Finally I had hooks or straps fastening practically everything.

I often wondered why Sweetie never got seasick. She certainly was a good sailor. Her favorite berth for the roughest rides seemed to be a little round basket into which she just fit. It was right in the middle of the trailer and always seemed to stay put where it sat on top of the electric oven in a corner of the kitchen. She was always in the best of health and spirits and would go on a wild tear up and down the length of the trailer every evening, soon learning how to upset my sewing box so she could chase the spools around. I couldn't leave my desk drawer open many minutes without having her lift most of the objects out and dump them on the floor. It was such fun to have her company in the trailer, and such fun to have that mischievous, affectionate, cuddly ball of husky puppy fluff riding with me in the jeep.

The snow came down and met me before that afternoon was over. Suddenly I could see no more than a very few feet in front of me. I knew I would have to pull off and park as soon as possible. But I couldn't see to the right or left and thought I'd never find a place. I knew it would be bad if darkness overtook me in such a blizzard.

I crawled along for many miles thinking I was going through flat desolate country. In reality I was passing magnificent mountains and a lake, drove right through an Indian settlement and passed several places I might have pulled off to park. But it was all I could do to keep on the road. Finally I could make out some dark objects which I knew to be one of the deserted army camps. I got out to investigate and to my surprise and joy saw smoke coming out of a chimney.

At the door I found a sign stating that it was the headquarters of the game warden. When I asked permission to park there Mr. Chambers said he was not allowed to permit any parking on those premises but no sooner were those words out of his mouth than he was showing me the best way to drive into the ground where I'd have a nice level parking spot protected from the worst winds and with plenty of room to circle around when it came time to leave.

"You shouldn't think of going further in this storm," he said. "It would be very dangerous, even for one familiar with the road. It has many sharp curves just ahead and winds along for many miles between the mountains and the water's edge."

I was so amazed when I woke in the morning to find myself in that dramatically beautiful spot on the shore of lovely Kluane Lake. And what a wonderful time little Peater was having in her first snow!

I had a grand time taking pictures and visiting with the very attractive wife of the warden. She had just recently come from Vancouver. Over at a desk in a corner of the living room sat a very handsome, very sober looking Indian boy, apparently studying. On my way out Mrs. Chambers whispered, "That boy's Indian mother just shot his white father yesterday so we're letting him stay with us a few days." The boy was taking a correspondence course in criminology.

September 26th seemed early to have real winter set in. They said there would be more warm, dry weather. A snowplow came by about noon. Kerosene or No. 1 distillate for my oil heater was difficult and frequently impossible to find. It was ranging from $1.00 to $1.50 a

gallon. I had been using my electric plant for heat but thought I'd give it a little rest this morning. I filled my oil stove with what the man at Morley River had sold me for No. 1 distillate. The stove refused to burn. I examined what was left in the can. It was nothing but rusty water! I siphoned out all I had put in the stove. Opened up the carburetor. It was full of water! What a mess. That stove was almost as difficult to take apart and put together again as the one in my old trailer It was an awful piece of junk which could not stand being hauled over any rough roads.

Snowstorm at Kluane, September 25, 1948

There was a little fountain of spring water in the warden's front yard. His job was supposed to have nothing to do with anything but game, poachers, etc., but all sorts of jobs were thrust upon him here such as looking for fires, helping countless vehicles that get stuck in places where the snow drifts very badly, looking after sundry emergencies, and now he had this half-breed Indian on his hands.

The Chambers had fixed up their house. It was very attractive and comfortable, including modern plumbing with gravity flow spring water just like I have on my Vermont farm except that they have to shut if off in winter. It's so cold there that no water can keep on running through any pipe.

When I left about two in the afternoon the snow had nearly melted off the road. It wasn't far to Burwash but I nearly missed it. It is down on the shore of the north end of Kluane Lake. I passed a road with a sign saying Burwash Hotel. Since I wasn't looking for a hotel I went on.

Finally I passed another road with a sign intended for those heading south. I had to back up and maneuver a difficult hairpin turn to get headed back. When I reached the village there was no possible space big enough for me to park or even room enough to turn around. If there hadn't been two roads leading into the place I'd still be there. Fortunately I was able to head out back to the highway on the road I had first seen with the hotel sign. I found a spot where it was wide enough to be safely off the highway.

Then I walked back down to have dinner and become better acquainted with the charming little village. Thought I might find some interesting people in the dining room. I had heard of Jene Jaquet, one of the real "characters" of the north country. He owned and operated the rustic inn which seemed to delight most tourists who stopped in. I guess he practically owned the town.

Some prosperous, ordinary, uninteresting and snooty tourists were seated at small tables. I readily accepted the suggestion that I sit at the sort of family table where Jene and his part Indian wife were eating, both so large that they occupied one whole side of a big table. Then there was the cook, the school teacher, a gold miner and two truck drivers. One of the drivers had passed me so many times on the highway it was like meeting an old friend.

Those who stuck to the job of driving huge transports up and down that road were doing it not just because they got well paid, but because it was a challenge. They derived a lot of satisfaction out of accomplishing something really difficult. They were not just thrill seekers but tough, capable, intelligent men. Such men have character and I found that most had a deep, aesthetic appreciation of the beauties of nature. They loved that highway. One said, "I get a new thrill out of every single mile on every trip I make." And he'd been plying that road for years.

When Jene introduced the miner, Henry Besner, he told me I'd be missing something if I did not visit the Besner mine up on Burwash Creek. Henry followed up with a cordial invitation. He said I could park my trailer on the highway just beyond the bridge which crossed the creek ten miles beyond Burwash Landing. I wanted very much to see an old-fashioned placer mine. They said Besner was one of the few successful operators. According to the stories, he kept bringing in quantities of gold — $10,000 worth a clip. They also told of his being one of the most successful gamblers in the famous ace-away game in Whitehorse. They said he would enter the game with $30,000 in his pocket. That was his limit. He would never allow himself to lose more than that. He usually finished the evening with more.

Interesting as the company was, I didn't stay very late. I knew I had a long walk through the dark black night to get back to my trailer. As I was leaving Barney whispered, "Do you like moose meat?" After my strongly affirmative answer, he led me out to a truck. Under a tarp he had a huge moose just bagged that afternoon. He cut out a five-pound chunk of tenderloin and handed it to me.

I enjoyed that walk alone back to the trailer. It was so dark I had to literally feel for the road—the kind of darkness when you can't see a thing if you look straight ahead, but if you look to the side, then, out of the corner of your eye you can get a faint impression of the direction of the road. With snow on the ground and dark trees along the side you would think you could see SOMETHING, but you couldn't, and I have good night vision. I never knew it could be SO DARK. I bumped into a couple of trees and just hoped a big bear wouldn't smell the moose meat and decide he wanted it more than I did.

That walk gave me a feeling of being so very close to the terrific bigness of that awe-inspiring country. Then when I stopped occasionally to get my breath in the climb, the world as a whole seemed so very small. Cities, even the biggest of them, seemed very small. International squabbles seemed so petty. Maybe if everyone could get away from everyone and everything once in a while, off in the wilds of the Yukon, it would be a good thing.

Pretty soon a delighted squeal from little Peater pierced the blackness and I knew the trailer was not far. I had used the chain the Teslin Mounty had given me to hitch her to the rear bumper so she could not follow me and maybe get herself mysteriously spirited away again.

Next morning it was pretty cold. The jeep started, ran a few seconds and then died. I found a solid mass of ice in the sediment bowl of the fuel pump. A nice road foreman came along, and then Barney Chesseaux. After cleaning the fuel pump, they found the gas line frozen. I thawed that out with my tiny alcohol blowtorch and put a pint of alcohol in the gas tank. Cars are heavy drinkers in the north country and will balk if you forget the alcohol.

Chesseaux was a very good mechanic. He also found the spark plugs in awful shape so I got out a new set and he put them in. He did some carburetor adjusting in the hope that I'd get better mileage. On the hard pulls I was getting barely five miles to the gallon. My gas bills were staggering. Instead of one or two dollars every time I stopped for gas I usually handed out somewhere between ten and twenty dollars. But don't forget I was carrying my hotel along with me.

I found the road leading in to the gold mine. The men sure were surprised when the jeep drove in sight.

They had a rough dam holding back part of the water of the stream. The bulldozer was scraping and pushing the muck, rocks and gravel, from the creek bed around to one side of a rack at the head of the sluice-box. The shovel would scoop it up and dump it on the rack of logs laid about six inches apart. The gravel, dirt and small stones would drop through into the sluice while Besner stood on the rack pushing the big rocks off to the side, a back-breaking job which the help couldn't be hired to do. So the boss did it himself. When the floodgate was open the water would rush through a large iron pipe and then wash down the sluicebox carrying off everything except the gold. Gold, being heavier than anything else, would drop to the bottom and get caught in the cracks in the boards at the bottom of the sluice.

They were working the dozer when I arrived. Their noon dinner hour was over, but when I told Besner I hadn't had anything to eat since breakfast he hustled me over to the cook shack for some tea and lunch.

Then I went back and scrambled over the icy rocks up and down the canyon to get pictures of all their operations. I slipped and fell flat on my back in about a foot of ice water, bruising and skinning my knee, cutting my left hand on sharp rocks But I held my Medalist camera up in my right hand so it did not get wet or bumped. I rolled over on my left side to climb out, forgetting that I had my Leica in my left pocket. The pocket was completely filled with water. I emptied it out, wiped off the Leica and finished shooting the roll. Not a single shot was spoiled and the camera was not damaged in the least. I wish that all cameras were made as well.

I got a thorough drenching, but my woolen clothes didn't remain cold or uncomfortable for long. When I got through taking pictures I went back to the cook shack where the cook made me some more hot tea and helped me dry out my shoes and socks. My sheepskin-lined boots had filled with water. Too bad none of the boys saw me on my back in the river—I must have made a picture.

Of course, I had to have supper with them—a fine meal. Wish my photograph of the bunch at the table had turned out better. It was one of the times when the Medalist did not function well.

I guess my visit was fun for them all. They'd never had a woman guest before. I wish I could have stayed to get pictures of them gathering the nuggets out of the sluice in the evening, but I was afraid I'd never be able to make the trip out of the place after dark So Peater and I hustled back to the highway, hitched up the trailer, and backed a few hundred feet to a good level place off the road to park for the night.

Just as I was getting things set and hooking up the light plant, the Mounty from Haines came along and said, "Well, you made only ten miles today."

21. THE FRIENDLIEST ROAD IN THE WORLD

I'd like to know just how many people along the highway, by that time, were keeping track of exactly where I was and what I was doing every minute. Instead of being off in a desolate and lonely place, as most of my friends and relatives thought, I was traveling the friendliest road in the world.

This Royal Canadian Mounty told me I'd find the surface and condition of the highway much better in Alaska than in Canada. I promptly sent this information from Canada back to Mrs. Charters in Grande Prairie where her paper had the audacity to print an article stating that Alaska was planning to hard surface the road, "being obliged to do so in order to bring their end of it up to that standard of maintenance being carried on throughout the Canadian section."

A little more than a hundred miles the next day brought me to the Canadian Customs at Snag in mid-afternoon. The officer, Frank Algar, had a husky pup named Peter who instantly became the best of rough and tumble friends with my Peater. An invitation was immediately extended to park on the other side of the office where an electric cord would reach through the window. Then an invitation to dinner in the mess hall of the maintenance camp. Then an invitation to attend the weekly movie which was to be shown that evening. All this before any of the Customs business was attended to, but that amounted to nothing but turning over the slips which had been given me when I entered Canada. The slips said something about permission to remain in Canada thirty days. They were dated July 11th and this was September 29th.

A very attractive young chap was doing the cooking in the mess hall and the food was fine. The movie was a good one, but a bit worn and scratched from its long trek up the highway with stopovers at every camp. The newsreel showed Ghandi making a speech and the ice jam in the Ohio River of the previous winter.

I guess everyone remembers when Snag broke all world records for cold with an official temperature of 83 degrees below zero three years ago. No thermometers were made to register that low but a bright young engineer rigged up a revised thermometer which was later sent to Washington. His reading was accepted as officially correct. There seems

Beyond
Muncho Lake

to be a pocket there where cold air settles. Nowhere in Alaska does it get so cold.

Next day I ate lunch in Alaska. I parked along side the road just beyond the sign marking the border and cooked myself a special meal to celebrate. Snag is about twenty miles below the border. The American Customs is at Tok Junction, a hundred miles beyond the border.

Sourdough Mountain presented me with a sudden STEEP hump which I did not succeed in making. I couldn't get a good run at it as they were working the road at both ends. A big grader pulled me up over the last few feet. They were obviously keeping the road in Alaska in much better shape than in Canada.

Then I stalled again on another steep pitch. A car from Texas came along straining itself on five cylinders and a burned out clutch. The driver stopped to see if he could help me. I appreciated the generous offer but wouldn't consider it. He then had to back up and try and try again before he finally succeeded in getting the car up over the top. As I sat there watching the struggle I thought for the thousandth time that the guy who said there was nothing more than a seven percent grade on that highway should be made to eat all the pamphlets in which that statement appears. I found plenty of road engineers and construction men who agreed with me that there were plenty of 27-percent grades.

The Alaska Highway Police Patrol finally came along. He said a maintainer would be along shortly. He waited till it came and then he saw how, when I pulled on alone, my front wheels came right off the ground. That made me realize I'd better add some more weight to help hold down the front end of the jeep so that I could get more out of the front wheel drive.

Four o'clock found me at such a nice place to park I decided to stop, even though I had covered only 30 miles. An up-and-coming young couple by the name of Seaton had built a very pretty modern little gas station and were planning cabins, trailer park and restaurant. There was a junk pile on their place where a lot of iron from an airport had been dumped. We hunted till we found just the thing to add to the front of my jeep—a big flat piece weighing about two hundred pounds.

Seaton fastened it on for me on top of the regular 250-pound jeep weight. It made a good shelf with a ridge along the front edge to hold things on. I found it swell for carrying a big bag of sand for even more weight and for use on icy hills. They would take no pay for the iron and gave me a discount on gas. They were so nice to me I wanted to buy something from them. Since they sold beer I conjured up enough thirst to get half a bottle down—50 cents, and the only bottle of beer I ever bought to drink myself in my whole life.

While I was drinking it the nice highway patrolman came in.

"Is dinner ready?" he asked.

"No, but give me about 20 minutes and I'll have a nice moose filet mignon ready."

He seemed to enjoy the moose and the conversation and was lots of fun. Before he left I happened to recall that my Vermont driver's license had expired the previous spring. I thought it would be fun to have an Alaska license. He said he'd be glad to give me one and got his briefcase out of his car with all the necessary papers. I filled out the blanks— life history, but not as bad as in some states. (Don't ever try to get one in Florida unless absolutely necessary. They'll flunk you there if you say a certain type of sign means to slow up—you should say "retard speed.")

I put down my age and date of birth on the application, showed him my old license which also stated my age, paid my dollar and got a nice new Alaska license which again made me a legal driver for awhile.

Since Mr. Seaton had had nothing but wire with which to fasten the big iron plate on the front of my jeep I was a bit worried for fear it might drop off and do serious damage. I kept looking for a place where I might fasten it more securely.

At Mile 1248 I stopped at the maintenance camp but none of the men were around. Those camp buildings all look alike—dull old olive drab barracks, but you never can tell what surprises you may find inside. When I knocked at a door at this camp I was greeted by a picture fit for a magazine cover. It would certainly be a brighter, happier world if all housewives might be caught in the middle of a busy morning in their kitchens looking as attractive as Mrs. Dewey Young, wife of the maintenance crew superintendent.

Her sweet cheerful face with its naturally pretty pink and white complexion, had as delicate an application of powder and make-up as though she had been just ready to step out to the opera. The glossy black curls of her hairdo were held in place with a bright blue ribbon and there was a riot of gay color in her becoming house dress and apron.

My next call, about 25 miles further up, was on Nell Kelly.

I don't mean to put Nell Kelly down as one of the worst, by any means. In many ways she's one of the best, I guess, but a greater contrast to Mrs. Young couldn't be found.

The day had hardly begun for Nell and if ever there was a good picture of "the morning after" she was the model for it. She was lounging bleary-eyed in a big old overstuffed chair by the stove in front of her bar with a book in one hand, a cup of strong coffee in the other and, her blonde hair straggling in every direction.

She runs a trading post in connection with her bar and a grocery store, and serves food when in the mood and when the dishes of previous meals finally get washed.

Nell has had many husbands. No one seems to know how many, or what happens to them all. The last they say was a sort of marriage of convenience whereby she acquired her present establishment. He seems to be out of the picture now. The words people hear her repeat most frequently are, "Well, I guess I'll get married again."

And she usually does. I didn't like to believe some of the stories I heard of how she acquired a good portion of her wealth by "rolling" the boys when they were drunk, but I do like to believe the stories of how many down-and-outers she has helped.

She certainly has many friends who think she has a heart as big as the whole north country. Her popularity brings a lot of the boys down the 60 miles from the Army base at Big Delta, and many drive the 160 miles from Fairbanks to pay her a visit. To me she was a rough, tough, likable old gal with whom I would have thoroughly enjoyed becoming acquainted.

Her fondness for animals was very deep. She fell terribly in love with my little Peater and wanted so much that I should let her buy her from me on my way back. She said I shouldn't take such a dog out of the north country because it would make such a valuable sled dog and also because it would have a much healthier, happier life up there where it was born and bred to live.

22. TOK TO FAIRBANKS

When I rolled up to the Customs Office at Tok a couple of tourist boys on their way south were just coming out. One of them held his hand above his eyes to scan the length of my outfit and then said gleefully to his partner, "Now I can go home happy—I've seen everything!" then the usual flood of questions as to how I ever got up the highway with such an outfit, and the dumb-founded surprise at finding I was doing it alone.

The police patrolman who had given me my license was there, and the good looking young customs officer started looking over all my papers in a very businesslike fashion. He had me fill out a lengthy questionnaire, show all my licenses, etc., and then asked me if I had a birth certificate.

The lists of regulations I had stated that no birth certificate was necessary to go through Canada or Alaska. Mr. Ahlen said he was sorry but it would be necessary for him to see it so he hoped I had it with me. I had fortunately brought an affidavit of my birth, along with my passport and all such papers. I told him I would look it up in my trailer. He said he would have to look through the trailer also.

When he got through looking over all the possible identification papers I could find, he said, "I hear you're a good cook—how about my bringing over a duck? If Laird enjoyed a dinner with you I don't see why I can't. He'll guide you over to a very nice place to park and I'll come by later. We can't let you go on further without stopping over to see our town."

I had told Laird, the police officer, about how my oil heater had fallen completely to pieces now so I couldn't use it at all. In the evening when he dined with me he saw what mess it was in and promised to have a good man there in Tok ready to fix it for me. As soon as he got me parked Abe came over with a portable workshop equipped for welding.

The work on the stove discombobulated the custom officer's plans for dinner. When he saw things torn up he said he'd drop by later after the office closed.

He wanted me to see his house. He was proud of having the only separate, individual house in the settlement. The inside was very artistically finished and furnished, quite modern, and very good taste.

Being very fond of good music he had a huge collection of fine records and was a fine dancer too. He was Scotch, born in Minnesota, lived in New York a good many years, and at the moment seemed to be thinking about nothing except getting married.

After we had danced and talked awhile, bringing up the subject of my age repeatedly, and asking questions galore about how old my son was, when I went to college, how old I was when I married, etc., he said, "Well, it's hard to believe, but I guess you're not a faker or a spy."

"I'll tell you the truth now about that birth certificate business. We thought you were traveling under false pretenses. Laird came into the office yesterday and said there was a woman coming up the highway alone with a huge trailer and that he was sure she wasn't within 15 years of the age she said she was. I gave her a driver's license. It checked up with her old license, but she may be travelling with someone else's papers. You'd better look her over carefully."

"When you took out your glasses saying, 'Grandma needs her specs to read this fine print,' I thought that might be a phoney remark, and then you remember I took your glasses out of your hand when you got through filling out the questionnaire. I looked through them expecting to find that they were just plain window glass. And of course the regulations don't require you to show a birth certificate unless you are under suspicion. We have to do what we can to help apprehend dangerous or subversive characters and we sure weren't going to let you go till we found out more about you. I'll tell you right here and now finding out about you is being a lot of fun."

"If you want to play fair you'll let me find out a lot about you too," said I, picking up a couple of photographs of girl friends from his table to scrutinize them carefully.

One girl friend was about to come up from New Rochelle to marry him recently. He had sent her a plane ticket and then she changed her mind and got mad because he told her she'd have to wait a couple more weeks in order to land at the Fairbanks airport which happened to be under water at the time. The other gal wanted terribly much to come up and marry him but he wasn't sure he liked her quite well enough.

"That's the way it goes, " I said, "You fall for the ones who don't like you well enough and don't love the ones who love you."

Then I told him a girl would have to care a lot for him to be willing to come away off up into that country to live with him. "It's a good test," I said, "because if a girl really loves a man she will be happy to be with him no matter in what godforsaken section of the world his work or his interests may keep him." Then I told him I thought that if a love affair did not shape itself toward matrimony with an exactly equal amount of love on both sides, which was rare, it would be safer to gamble with the woman having the greater portion of love to give.

"You're a selfish individual," I said, "and it's going to take a lot of tolerance and generosity on the part of the woman who marries you."

"What's more," I said, "you'd better hurry up and get married. There's nothing more uninteresting than a confirmed bachelor, and there's something wrong with a man who hasn't got what it takes to gamble on marriage at least once."

Then he kept recounting the pros and cons of the New Rochelle girl and the pros and cons of the other who was a nurse, not so pretty, but a very sweet, lovable girl with a wonderful character. However the other was much more exciting. I told him he was such an attractive male he had been spoiled by women, was accustomed to getting what he wanted, and was now intrigued by one who had turned him down.

"You know—there's something about you," he said "and not only look a lot like the New Rochelle girl but you are like her."

"At least twice her age, I imagine."

"To hell with your age!" Then he told me about Laird's wife being older than he and how happy their marriage was turning out to be.

"What's more," he said, "Here you are—you came up into this country all on your own. No one asked you to come, or brought you or forced you to come. There aren't many women who would think of coming this far up into such country. You must like it or you would have turned back long ago. Most of the girls these boys send for to come up here to marry them hate it when they get here and either leave or make life very miserable for their husbands while they stay here."

"So you think I should stay and marry you."

"Well, I tell you, there's certainly something about you—lots of things that appeal to me. Tear up that affidavit of your birth and begin putting yourself down as 15 or even 18 years younger and you can get by with it."

"When you're 55, I'll be 70. You probably wouldn't be able to see that 'something' then."

Six months later Jerry was happily married to the nice little nurse.

A new Spartan trailer was parked near me, an elderly couple who live near my aunt and uncle in California. I had met then in Athabasca. They had made the trip successfully pulling the light Spartan with a new Cadillac. They were waiting here for another couple with a trailer who were traveling along with them but were delayed with a lot of tire and wheel trouble. They finally broke a trailer axle between Anchorage and Tok. The couple in the Spartan were suffering with the cold as there were no electric hookups and the heater in their trailer was a gasoline stove which would not operate without an electric blower. I hooked them up to my electric plant.

When the people with the other trailer arrived they had a lot of grouse they had shot along the road. They gave me one and took the others out back of the Spartan to dress out. The rest of the day little Peater kept coming back from the Spartan, so fat she could hardly waddle and with so many feathers sticking to her she looked like some strange four-legged bird.

I went into the store and bought an apple for 25¢, a peach for 24¢ a piece of squash for 38¢ a pound.

Since Abe was such a good mechanic I wanted him to weld the hitch back on the front end of the jeep and do the necessary work on my extra iron weight. He had to do the work after hours in the evening. That meant I could enjoy a leisurely day around Tok. Maybe I shouldn't have said no to a party that evening but I thought the only entertainment would probably be drinking. Instead I invited Abe to bring his little wife in for a visit.

They were a nice couple. They had brought a truck and trailer to try their luck at living in Alaska. And they had the most sincere admiration for Nell Kelly. It seems their outfit went to pieces when they got as far as her place. She took them in, provided them with food and quarters till they got on their feet, insisting that they owed her nothing. They said they would be eternally grateful to her and they knew she had helped many others in a similarly gracious manner allowing them to feel no indebtedness or obligation.

Next morning Jerry was so nice about helping me get filled up with gas and water and took me around to the maintenance camp where he checked all my tires — no small job with my outfit, and they had to be kept just right. By then it was noon and he insisted on cooking a fine lunch for me before I started out. He'll make a pretty good husband.

It didn't take long to cover the 112 miles to Big Delta that afternoon. The country was flat and uninteresting, just a couple of hills leading up from two fine bridges across Robertson and Johnson rivers.

Laird, the highway policeman, had described them to me and I found him waiting there to make sure I made it. He had told the folks at at Triangle Lodge at Big Delta to expect me. So I received a warm welcome and was hooked up to their electricity (without charge). I felt obliged to have dinner in their restaurant. $3.50 for chicken fried in fat so rancid I couldn't eat it.

There were lots of men from the Big Delta army base hanging around the bar drinking. Getting into conversation with one I said, "I don't like military bases." A fellow lolling over in a corner, smashed his bottle of beer down on the table and yelled, "You can say that again, lady." It was no atmosphere for me so I cleared out and went to bed.

Next morning at breakfast I got the story from Luke and Jean Riley as to how they happened to land there. They were making loads of money in their very attractive looking place.

They had left New Mexico in May of 1946 with a car and small luggage trailer. They didn't like Fairbanks, so they sold their car and bought a thirty-foot river boat with a 22-horse outboard motor. They started down the Yukon with only a few cents left and enough grub to last a few weeks. Opening a can of sardines on July 9th, Jean cut her wrist in such a way as to nearly scare the life out of both of them. They were sure she would bleed to death. The first sign of any habitation they found was a place called Ruby where they got some first aid for the cut wrist.

Luke asked some of the drunken Indians who were hanging around where they got their liquor. They all complained about having to go so very far in order to get it. "All right," said Luke, "I'll bring it to you."

Everyone fell to help him build a log cabin bar and restaurant which he opened for business in September. Goodness knows how much he made selling liquor that winter. He sold the place in June, went back to Fairbanks, bought a fine car, took a 15,000-mile tour back through the states, returned and lived in Fairbanks in style the following winter and then decided to locate at Triangle. Here he built his fine looking place at a very strategic spot where the Richardson Highway from Anchorage comes in to meet the road from Fairbanks. To say he is doing well would be putting it mildly.

The one hill left between here and Fairbanks was the steepest of the entire highway and everyone had been telling me that if I had needed help on any of them I'd never make Shaw Creek Hill. The police, the customs and the road men all said I couldn't do it, and there were several truck drivers in the Triangle Lodge that morning at breakfast telling how difficult it was. Some of them said they were never able to get their trucks up over without the help of a cat.

There was one old trucker who had passed me several times along the way. He said quietly to me on the side, "I think you can do it if you throw'er in the cellar and rev'er full blast BEFORE you ever start the climb no matter how she roars and no matter what your rules say about not going over eight or nine in low . Give'er all she's got even before you get over the bridge 'cause she starts going straight up at the other end."

Half a dozen people were making themselves available to help me. I was intending to stop at the maintenance camp near the bridge and let someone from there pull me up over but my desire to show'em all I COULD do it got the best of me when I looked down upon the bridge. I saw the hill looming up ahead and I had a hunch I might do it by following the old driver's advice.

When I zoomed up over the top I let out a few squeals of joy, got out and danced around with little Peater who joined in my glee with all her peppy puppy enthusiasm. I told her I thought we might have made all the hills of the highway on our own if we had been sufficiently warned. But there was an important factor which helped in climbing this one — the roadbed was perfect. Had there been any loose gravel or sand we never could have done it. It was the rough, hard packed crushed stone on the steepest curves and that gave the best possible traction.

Soon as I found a good place to park, I cooked the grouse for lunch to celebrate.

Then the country leveled out again in the uninteresting looking valley of the Tanana River. It was getting dark but I could tell I was passing near huge air bases and military camps as I approached Fairbanks. The last ten miles seemed never ending with a tremendous amount of traffic and choking dust on the loose, crushed stone laid in preparation for the hard surfacing.

There were several large trailer parks just outside Fairbanks. I pulled into the Arctic Village which had been recommended. The wife of the proprietor, who looked as though she might have been in the Ziegfield Follies, welcomed me and pointed out a vacant parking lot. It was a very tiny spot and there was no one to help guide me into it in the dark. So, all by myself, I had to back and maneuver and maneuver and back, getting out every foot or so to see where the rear end of the trailer was going. After I got all set and was unhitching people began to come around and no one could understand how I ever got in there.

23. FAIRBANKS

It snowed all night but melted away fast the next day. It was a surprise to see what a big modern city Fairbanks was. It had some fine buildings, paved streets, parking meters, some women dressed ala Sax Fifth Avenue, some characters it would take chapters to describe, and groups of Eskimos in their fantastic costumes waiting for busses.

The parking meters gave you 15 minutes for five cents and I got a ticket right off the bat. I told the traffic office we were much more polite to our guests in Vermont by giving them a nice little warning tag for the first offense which said WELCOME in big letters and then gently informed of the violation. They saw nothing interesting or amusing in that and then they all went into a dither when I demanded a receipt for my dollar. They said they never gave receipts. I finally got one.

Then I went to the bank. I had just six dollars left. I asked about wiring my bank to send some money to the bank there so I could get some travelers checks. That was simple enough, but then I asked whether they would be willing to cash a small check for me so I could get along until the money arrived. In spite of all the identification, credit cards, a letter from my lawyer stating that he had deposited some money to my account—nothing could persuade them to risk cashing a check. Finally the gentleman I was talking to took a $10 bill from his pocket and insisted upon my taking it. I didn't know I was talking to the president of the bank, Mr. Stroker.

At the general delivery desk in the post office they had no mail for me. That I could NOT understand. Something must have gone radically wrong. There should have been a huge collection awaiting me. Several times before I had used Fairbanks as a forwarding address and then when delayed for weeks or months somewhere I had written and asked them to send it back down which they had always done promptly. Though I had tried to have it all marked "hold" this time, I was afraid they had returned it all to the senders. When I called again next morning I was presented with a grand big stack which the lady said had "just arrived." The general delivery desk handles a terrific amount

Second Avenue, Fairbanks, 1948. 6,000 miles and I got a parking ticket right off the bat.

of mail and there are always two long lines of people calling for it.

Before that first day ended the possibilities of a job were mentioned to me—something to do with the radio department of the Lathrop Enterprises. Did I want a job? I certainly could not stay up there any length of time without one. Salaries sounded high but I soon found that the cost of living was so completely beyond all reason that some of the people there with supposedly well-paid positions were having a terrible struggle to make ends meet. There were so many cases where people were pathetically stuck. They hated it there but couldn't get a cent ahead to get themselves out and back down to the states again.

I had heard that federal bureaucracy and some shocking monopolies carried on by one or two Seattle families were to blame for conditions in Alaska. Why should those Seattle steamship companies charge a rate twice that of any other ocean hauls? Why should the ten-mile rate on the Alaska Railroad be eight times that of the average freight line in the United States? Why should it cost as much to send a parcel post package a distance of 14 miles in Alaska as it does to send the same package from Boston to Los Angeles?

The Seattle family owns the fisheries and canneries, pays Alaska no taxes, transports its own labor to and from Alaska on its own ships, and sells a can of salmon to an Alaskan resident for a high price plus freight both ways since the can has been boated to Seattle for labeling.

The fisheries are Alaska's most valuable industry though a very small portion of it belongs to Alaska. And I heard much talk about how, unless some control is put into force, there will soon be no more fish.

We often hear of the limitless wealth of resources and read of Alaska's comparing favorably with Norway and Sweden. One old timer didn't seen to agree. Mr. Anderson calls it the Land of the Spitting Spud. He says they claim to grow good potatoes but no matter how he cooks one, when he sticks a fork into it to see if it's done, it spits at him.

To him, Alaska is bound on the north by Stephanson, on the east by Perdition, on the west by Bolshevism, and on the south by Applications for Government jobs. But he says it has only three sides: Inside, Outside and Morningside. Morningside, it seems, is the bug house. "Outside" is the word everyone hears right and left. No one ever goes "to the states" or "back home"—if he leaves Alaska, no matter whether it's always "Outside."

As for the other resources, Mr. Anderson told me they were over-rated. He says most people have come to realize that gold is not of good enough quality to pay to mine it. It usually takes an enormous investment to set up operations—more than the small returns can warrant.

Except for pulpwood, he says there is no timber except on the Panhandle, and he claims that is not of good quality. The coal, he thinks, is inferior. He says they may find oil worth going after in the north. There is no waterpower in winter. Trapping he considers a waste of time since fur can be grown for a third the cost on farms in the northern states.

But Mr. Anderson has been in Alaska most of his life and I don't think anything can induce him to go "outside." When I asked him why he stayed there he couldn't seem to think up an answer.

There were many hale, hearty and active old people in Alaska. Maybe it is the survival of the fittest and in order to survive you have to be so damn fit nothing can kill you off.

Having become acquainted with Cap Lathrop I knew I couldn't leave Alaska without a photograph of him. I heard he was leaving Fairbanks for a few days so I got up at the crack of dawn to catch him as he was boarding the early morning train to go down to his mines. He had been up practically all night celebrating his 84th birthday. He sure is still going strong, and what a twinkle in his eye!

No one knows Alaska who doesn't know Cap Lathrop, and if it were not for him Alaska certainly would not be what it is. He looks like a sourdough prospector, hates to dress up and is never happier than when doing a good day's dirty hard work in his coal mine. "Alaska's only home-grown millionaire," is what George Nelson Meyers calls the richest man in the Territory, and then goes on to explain that he does not catch salmon, trap mink or pan gold.

Lathrop builds, makes money and invests his profits in more building. Everything which is well built, all the fine, modern, concrete buildings, seem to have been built by and belong to Cap—a chain of moving picture houses, hotels, apartment houses, offices, banks, etc.

He is president of and heaviest investor in two banks, publishes the farthest north daily newspaper, and his radio station is the farthest north commercial broadcasting outfit in the world. When he built the Lacy Street Theater in Fairbanks it was the most expensive movie house per seat ever constructed in the United States. Now the new theater in Anchorage is even finer.

He has excellent taste and is helped in all details of planning, decorating and furnishing by his most capable and efficient secretary, Miriam Dickey who makes frequent trips to Seattle and Hollywood and does what she can to keep a high class selection of pictures coming to the theaters. Cap does not gouge the public as others do. The rents in his apartments and hotels are in line with what the same quarters would be in the states. You would pay two or three times as much for a room in a dirty old fire-trap as you would pay for a clean modern room in one of Cap's building —if you could get in.

At Suntrana he has developed the Healy River veins into the largest coal mine in the Territory and, according to Meyers, Cap became a vital figure with the Japanese in the Aleutians threatening the Alaska sea lanes. The Army had to have Cap's coal—trying days for him. "The Army was hollering for more coal this morning," he would say. "This afternoon they drafted four more of my miners."

When I asked Cap what he thought about Alaska becoming a state he said he was sure it would eventually, but he did not feel it was quite ready for statehood yet. I wonder whether, by any chance, he was thinking of the taxes he would have to pay. If it does become a state I wish Cap's enterprises might be allowed to carry on tax free. I think he deserves a bonus for having done so much for Alaska. I hope to get another picture of him on his 104th birthday still carrying on full blast.

Most folks go to Alaska to get rich quick and return to the states. (They usually do neither.) But when Cap saw Alaska he liked it and decided to stay.

One of the men in Alaska who first began to think about, talk about and work for a highway to that corner of the continent, is Donald McDonald. When they built the highway they did not follow the route he had in mind.

He did not want it to go through the more level country to the east of the Rockies, cutting over through the Peace River country as it does. He wanted it to cut through the mountains near the coast via a shorter route to Seattle. He claims his route would have saved 1000 miles to Seattle and 200 miles to Chicago. He is fanatically opposed to the present route, sits up there in his Fairbanks office and rants and raves and runs for political office and says the present highway should be immediately abandoned. He claims they built it with no intelligent planning and that all it is good for is to service the airports which are strung along near it.

I asked him whether he didn't think the airports were very important. He said they could build roads to the inferior from his route to service these airports. That would mean a good many miles of difficult and expensive road building, if you ask me. The thing to do is someday have both routes. And, again, what advantages could be derived all around if boundaries could only be wiped out and all the great northwest section of Alaska, Canada and the U.S. be one country with a network of roads leading in every direction for whatever the various sections may have to offer in the way of resources? The Peace River country sorely needs both rail and truck routes to the west coast.

Had I been able to get a job with the Extension Service I might have settled down there for a year or so, in order to get to really know Alaska.

I looked up the Extension Service director at the University which is located at the town of College a few miles north of Fairbanks. Mr. Oldroyd said he wished I had put in an appearance before the harvest was over. He would have had some work for me to do in the Matanuska Valley, but now there would be nothing worth photographing till the growing season again got into swing in the spring.

I tried to get myself invited to the Sourdough Pie Supper, an annual affair which any Cheechako (new comer) would give a lot to attend. Mr. Oldroyd had told me I ought to see it and he felt sure Eva McGown could get me in. But Miss McGown couldn't find a way in spite of the fact that she seemed to be the one person in Fairbanks who could accomplish the impossible.

She was one of the "characters" and sat at a desk in the lobby of the Nordale Hotel putting in about sixteen hours out of every twenty- four finding places for desperate people to live. Maybe you couldn't always call them places, but she never seemed to fail to find some sort of temporary shelter. And that was SOMETHING. If anyone thinks he has ever seen or heard of any housing shortage he has no idea of what it can mean without visiting Alaska.

The one good hotel and the other old but fairly decent place were always full and never known to observe any requests for reservations. If you knew the right people and happened to be standing at the desk waiting when someone checked out you might be able to get in.

According to Dr. Joseph W. Mountain of the U.S. Public Health Service, many communities in the Territory will not be able to expand until they get a good water supply and sewage disposal system. He claims the present housing inadequacy is definitely contributing to health problems in Alaska. Water purification and sewage systems used in the states won't work in permanently frozen ground.

I remember seeing the biggest hot water tank you could imagine in Jerry Ahlen's house in Tok—it must have held a thousand gallons and was run by oil heat which in turn meant a huge consumption of fuel. I said, "You're a big man but do you need all that hot water for a shave and a shower?" He explained that most of that hot water had to be kept circulating through pipes which ran underground all the way from his house to the source of his cold water supply. A hot water pipe ran along each side of the cold water pipe in a tunnel in order to keep the cold water from freezing.

And the water supply in Fairbanks was the worst I ever encountered. Except in Cap Lathrop's buildings and a few others who had their own private supply, the city water was not fit to use for ANYTHING. Its color was almost a chocolate brown. After a shower in it you were so rusty your joints would squeak. You couldn't possibly wash any clothes in it unless you wished to dye a pair of stockings a darker shade, and I wouldn't want to use it for cooking. It camouflaged beverages so you couldn't tell whether you were drinking tea or coffee.

The Alaska Housing Authority owns a community barracks building where it rents 60 10' x 12' rooms at $60 a month and six slightly larger rooms for $82.50. Sixty-eight families wait in line to cook on two hot plates and two stoves and use three sinks. The laundry has one washing machine and one double laundry tub. The men's latrine has four toilets and showers and five wash basins.

Some military personnel are paying exorbitant rentals for crude board or tarpaper shacks with dirt floors in order to have a little privacy. A 2nd Lt. pays $150 per month for two rooms, 8 x 10 and 10 x 12 with no water or bath. A Ssgt. with his family of three pays $110 a month for a one room 9 x 13 shack where 66 families, all with at least one child, use a community bath house containing three toilets, two showers and two wash basins for men and two toilets, two showers, two basins for women.

A captain and family spent a winter in an old GI vehicle crate. He is now terribly lucky to have a log cabin with three rooms, chemical toilet, no water, and at $85 a month—one of the real bargains.

One man was allowed to move into half a house by paying a whole year's rent in advance to the tune of $1500. And I found a listing which stated that one could have a room in a barracks out on a 17th Street for $5 a day—"Female roomers engaged in questionable enterprises."

Questionable enterprises on "The Line," Fairbanks

There was a big to do about the famous "Line" of which Fairbanks has always boasted. It was a long block of small shacks and cabins behind which ran a fine big wide alley. Each girl paid $700 a month rent for her house, and was said to make between $2000 and $3000 a month. Each

one paid a handsome price for coal, milk, telephone, electricity, etc. Good business for the various industries and utilities. Each girl was supposed to report every so often for medical checkup and get a receipt for some sort of vagrancy fine, all of which made it very legal.

The Line did not appeal to General Gaffney. He demanded that it be closed. Fairbanks refused. He threatened to put the entire city off limits. Still they refused. He stationed guards at each end of the alley. He again threatened to put the city off limits. A very large proportion of the city's business comes from the military. The Line was finally closed — that is, the girls all moved to other quarters.

Some residents of the town didn't quite like it now that they apparently have questionable enterprises going on in their swank sections. In fact Fairbanks as a whole is much displeased by General Gaffney's interference. But they've named a street after him.

When I saw an extremely well dressed woman on the street I usually suspected she was one of the girls from the Line. Most of them are said to finally settle down in marriage with the man of their choice and with ample fortune to get him well started in some very successful business. And Fairbanks had the Line long before it had the military.

I learned a lot about Fairbanks from a grand little lady, Henrietta McKaughan, who was a very important part of *Jessen's Weekly* which calls itself "Alaska's Leading Newspaper" and sports seven comic strips — four of them Cicero's Cat and the other three Mutt and Jeff. Henrietta put in a nice long story about me crowding most of my life history into a couple of columns. To my surprise she got most of it right—had no idea she was making so many mental notes when she was entertaining me at a delightful dinner and evening in her apartment. You have to be careful about what you say to these newspaper people.

It was funny hearing myself talked about on the radio one evening when a voice said, "A traveler that has seen more of Alaska than many Alaskans is Iris Woolcock, free-lance photographer and writer, etc." And the trailer, as usual, described as "a dream of every traveler."

It was so cold and dark and dreary every day in Fairbanks I kept thinking the long winter night was approaching. But the sun came out the morning of October 11th and made a fairly normal day out of it though it was shorter than we're accustomed to for that time of year in the states.

I kept missing calls and messages from a Lt. Goodyear so I started out to try to find him at Ladd Field. What an experience that was! After getting permission to go by the guards at the gate and having them try to locate the lieutenant's whereabouts and give me directions as to where I might find him, I drove for miles on paved highways. I had a very hard time making myself realize I wasn't lost out on Long Island.

But I sure was lost in Ladd Field—and it's not one of the really large bases in Alaska. I drove from one corner to another and from one hangar to another and never did find the lieutenant. The next day I found him in a trailer across the road from where I was parked!

He and his wife and two babies were living in a small trailer in a terrible trailer park. The trailer had rolled over on their way up with it, practically demolishing it and all their possessions, but the Lieutenant had done an expert job of rebuilding it. Lucky he was the kind who could do it or he and his lovely little family would have been in a still worse predicament with no place to live.

I was beginning to be a bit embarrassed by the way my trailer began to look. I just couldn't keep up with Peater who had reached the age where she thought the thing to do was drag home anything and everything she could possibly find in the community. There was a perfectly good GI raincoat. There were the usual towels and rugs and aprons with considerable wear left in them, and there were countless objects which had evidently been discarded and hauled from some dump.

Determined to visit the Canaday family, I pulled out the morning of the 14th. I figured the ground was frozen hard enough for me to haul the trailer over the muddy corduroy road which led from the highway to their house. Edna and L. Moore Canaday had always liked country living and had done some farming in the state of Washington. They knew it would take a lot of hard work to carve something for themselves out of the cold wilderness of Alaska but the north country appealed to them so they made the move.

Not having money to acquire equipment and get their buildings up L. Moore had to take a job working on the road and do his building in his spare time. The two sons, Brene, about 30, and his younger brother Elmore, staked claims adjoining their father's land. Mr. Canaday had taken his time and had been extremely careful in making an intelligent selection of land. There seems to be little help available in Alaska for those who seek advice in choosing good land for agriculture.

By following a brook down to where it emptied into the Tanana and finding considerable deposits of rich topsoil, he then followed it back upstream, looking for the land from which the good soil had washed. He traced out small irregular sections where the frost thawed out during the brief summer season. Some of his nearest neighbors have spent a lot of money building very nice homes only to find they can't grow a thing on their land. They put a carrot seed in the ground and it doesn't want to grow down toward that horribly cold chunk of frozen tundra. It just sends out a few roots straggling sideways and is a total failure.

The first year their garden was a failure. Canaday's thought the fresh soil would not need any fertilizer, but it needs something to free the nitrogen. It has been frozen so long there is no free nitrogen and they have to use some general fertilizer because of a potash deficiency.

After the Canaday's raised some nice tomatoes, the old county agent paid them a visit and, looking right at the beautiful red tomatoes said, "You can't raise tomatoes up here."

The Canadays

Real homesteaders who are making a good go of it. No help and no money to start with.

L. Moore built a big hothouse for starting things and has made an underground storage house so they can keep on supplying the markets with fine fresh vegetables long after the harvest. Their produce is always in great demand.

The difficulty in raising cabbages is to keep them small enough for market. If not controlled, they get to 20, 30, or even 40 pounds. When things grow in Alaska, they grow fast. Since Canadays can't count on rain during their growing season, they have rigged up an efficient irrigation system.

L. Moore, being very clever and inventive, has made his one small tractor pinchhit for every conceivable type of machinery he needs on the farm. He hitches it up to one end of a long saw rig he invented. Then he sits at the other end and turns a crank and out come beautiful boards of any size or shape he might need.

At the moment he was building a third room on the log house. It had the typical roof best suited for the north country and made of poles covered with a layer of heavy paper, then 18 inches of moss, then six inches of dirt with split spruce boards to top it off. Instead of making roofs for the snow to slide off as we do, they make them with a low pitch to encourage the snow to remain on to give them added insulation against the winter's cold.

The cache was just about the most important of the out buildings. It stood high off the ground on sturdy log stilts banded with metal to discourage the mighty marauders intent on chewing it down. In the cache were kept the dry groceries and frozen meat. It had to be a good size in order to accommodate anything more than the yearly moose which would give them a minimum of 800 to 1,000 pounds of meat.

The Canadays were very disappointed in the failure of their female husky to produce pups. They looked longingly upon Peater, fully aware of the fact that she had been so beautifully bred with all the points most desired for the perfect sled dog. I realized that no people could love their dogs more and threat them more wonderfully than these people. This was the loveliest home I could ever possibly find for my darling adorable little Peater. If I were ever going to part with her it had better be now or never.

A few months before Mrs. Canaday had come home with a little pup she had found injured and deserted alongside the road. She still felt sad because she had not been able to save it.

"I would so love to have a dog I could call mine," she said. "Jack is Brene's dog and Judy belongs to L. Moore." So after seeing and hearing them repeatedly say how much they wished they might some-day have a pup like Peater, I laid the big ball of soft, silky, affection-ate, irresistible fluff in Mrs. Canaday's arms and drove off — quick.

I was glad I didn't know how she ran from window to window crying and finally found a bench from which she could strain her little eyes and ears for the last of the disappearing jeep and trailer, her baby heart completely broken at being left behind. Would that animals could only understand the well-meaning intentions and actions on the part of their masters or mistresses.

When I flew back to Alaska and saw Peater five months later she was a magnificent big gold and white creature weighing about 80 pounds and extremely happy in her grand home. She had apparently forgotten all about me and was fully engrossed in her duties as watch dog for the premise. They said she was so intelligent she didn't need to be taught anything and showed great talent for work in the harness she adored.

Her coat was exquisite and I realized what a shame it would have been to have brought her down out of the north country.

24. PHOTO SHENANIGANS

Since I did not want to take time to develop a lot of film, I wrapped up a large package to send to Pavelle in New York. The difficulty of getting film or negatives in and out of Canada had kept my first day in Fairbanks busy. I walked past a photographic shop where they had some very good work displayed in the window. I went in to talk with the proprietor, a Mr. Griffin. He said if I wished to have him develop my film he could do it himself in fine grain developer and take every precaution to turn out careful work for me at the same price I would pay in New York. This seemed a simple solution which would save me a lot of time and the trouble of trying to figure out where I would be when the film was ready to be returned to me from New York. I left the entire batch with him.

When I called next day he had finished the 2 1/4 x 3 1/4 rolls and they were in envelopes of individual frames. They were well developed but I was surprised to find a good many blanks among them. My Medalist camera was proving unreliable and although it sometimes turned out some poor work, I was unaccustomed to getting blanks. When I held two or three up in a certain light there was a barely discernable image or some child I had no recollection of ever having seen. Dope that I am, I threw away all the blanks without further scrutiny which might have shown me that the blanks did not have the little pattern of light leak which marked the upper margin of all my Medalist shots.

Next day Mr. Griffin said he had not yet finished my 4 x 5 negatives. "Are you sure you did not give me a new package of 4 x 5 film by mistake?"

"Why no, I have my boxes carefully marked," I said.

"But this box has all the film packed with the black paper between each sheet."

"Of course," said I, "I never store or pack film for shipping without paper to protect it."

"I suppose a woman would," said he, "but I have a feeling as I handle it in the darkroom that I am handling a box of new and unused film."

"But I'll have them ready if you call back tomorrow."

Next day he said, handing me package, "I was right. You'll do well if you can find a picture on that batch of film."

I should have asked him where my box was. This was merely wrapped in tinfoil and paper, and as I looked at the sheets of blank film it somehow did not look or feel quite natural to me. The notching code was all the same and didn't seem familiar. I told him I thought I had used two or three different types of film in the batch.

"You must have switched boxes," he said.

I went back to the trailer and carefully examined my boxes of film all carefully marked with the number of sheets removed, and my film holders all marked with the type of film with which they were loaded. I took the boxes which had been opened but which I felt sure contained unused film — how could I take a chance and use it? I MUST have made some mistake. He developed it all. Another batch of blanks. Then I unloaded all my film holders. I might have loaded them with the exposed film. He developed another batch of blanks.

"Maybe your camera isn't working. Sometimes shutters are affected by the cold."

"Yes, but many of those pictures were taken where it was warm."

I tried out the never failing Speed Graphic. It was certainly working.

"I DON'T understand this," I said. "Are you sure you did not make some mistakes in your darkroom? You might have put that first batch of film in the hypo first or something of the sort."

"Oh no, we have a very well laid out work room where it would hardly be possible to make such a mistake."

"Well," said I, "Someone has obviously made a very serious mistake. When my 4 x 5 Kodachrome is finished I'll know whether the camera was working. I took many of those shots in color at the same time."

"Oh did you?" he said, turning toward the shelf of film back of the counter. "Here, take this new package of black and white —it's the type you use mostly, isn't it? I only wish there were something more I could to do help. Of course none of us is infallible and if it is our mistake I certainly am sorry."

"Those negatives were my best and most dramatic shots of the highway and some of them were pictures taken for certain important uses. It means a terrible loss to me."

"But you have all those 2 1/4 x 3 1/4 negatives," he said and then went on asking me questions as to how I got some of my dramatic cloud effects, what filters I used, etc.

I felt pretty sick.

Before I left Canaday's I told L. Moore about it. He is quite a photographer. "That man has stolen a lot of good negatives," he said. "There is such a demand for pictures of the highway and Griffin needs thousands of postcards to keep that rack of his full. The tourists pay good prices for good enlarged photographs."

But again, dope that I am, I hadn't worked up enough suspicion of crooked work and had no proof. However, I had not thrown away that batch of blank 4 x 5s.

The day I left Canaday's I drove down the road wondering whether I could possibly find proof that Griffin had kept my negatives. I took time enough while parked beside the road for lunch to get out those first blank negatives and examine them further. I had my entire photographic library with me and could look up practically anything. In my Photo-Lab-Index I succeeded in locating the notching code on these sheets of film. To my utter horror and amazement it was film I had never bought, possessed or used — Kodak Infrared.

It was a good thing that I had eaten a hearty lunch before I made the discovery. I was fairly trembling with rage when, a few miles further down the road I met my old friend the police patrol. Laird was on his way to Fairbanks with an alcoholic. "I'm not surprised," he said, "I told you when I first met you that there was a scarcity of good pictures of the highway."

Then he said he'd have the police in Fairbanks speak to Griffin. I told him that whatever he did I hoped it wouldn't spoil my chances of getting those negatives.

When I reached Triangle Lodge I put in a person-to-person call to Griffin. When he answered I didn't ask him whether he had found my negatives. I didn't give him the chance to say a word till I had said, "YOU HAVE MY NEGATIVES. You substituted some old Kodak Infrared film. I have never owned any Infrared. I WANT MY NEGATIVES! Then he said, "Oh yes, I found your negatives just after you left and didn't know what to do with them or where to send them." (Everyone in Fairbanks knew exactly where I was every minute.)

Then, again being the prize dope of all dopes, I told him I'd appreciate it if he would air mail them to Whitehorse where I could pick them up with my other mail in about a week. Anyone else would have had sense enough to have some trustworthy friend call for them.

They were not in Whitehorse when I called for my mail. I wrote him. No reply. Weeks and months passed. I wrote a very hot letter telling him he had not heard the end of the episode. After four months a note came to me from the Ansco Company telling me they had received FROM me a package of processed black and white film and asking what to do with it. I had never sent any film, color or otherwise, to the Ansco Company. When they mailed the package to me — there it was — not all of it, and some very peculiar looking negatives. They were shots

I had taken along scenic Marsh Lake where the highway skirts at the foot of dramatic mountains. I had remembered waiting a night there to get pictures when the sun was shining. These shots were all mottled and my cloud effects nearly obliterated. What had happened to them was beyond me.

I sent them to be analyzed by an expert in New York. The report came back that they were not original negatives but copies made through frosted glass.

When I went back up to interview the military and city housing authorities I called on Griffin. He was an important member of the city council and the probable next mayor of Fairbanks, and after all, one mustn't be suspicious of anyone like that.

"You must have thought me a crook," said he.

"Oh no," said I

"Of course we all do have careless help and can't watch them carefully enough," said he.

"Of course," said I.

25.   TIME TO HEAD SOUTH

The afternoon of the day I left Canaday's the snowy road began to get very slippery. I didn't relish the idea of going down Shaw Creek Hill. On ice it would have been suicide to attempt that terribly steep road winding around sharp curves with the mountain up on one side and a thousand-foot drop off below. I finally caught up with a road scraper and though it was going only four miles an hour I followed it for many miles. It was giving me a rough gravel surface to drive on.

About three o'clock, a short ways before we reached the hill, it stopped and the driver came back to talk. He said he had to run and go back to his camp and told me I mustn't dare go down Shaw Creek until next morning when he would be back about ten o'clock. He said he'd have another man and machine with him and that one of them would hook on the front of me and the other would hook on the back of me and they would see to it that I got saafely down the hill. He told me to park right there where I was beside the road until they came for me.

A knock on the door later in the evening. It was Laird stopping in for a visit. WHAT A FRIENDLY ROAD! A wonderful road and wonderful people. I loved every inch of it.

The next morning the two huge graders came. I moved along with them to the crest of the hill where they had intended to hook on. We could look down on the slope from there and we saw that the sun had hit that side of the mountain warmly enough to take all the ice off. So they watched me go down safely by myself.

When I walked into the Triangle Lake Lodge to phone back to Fairbanks that day there were, as usual, several uniforms at the bar. They were pouring over a newspaper. Luke the bartender said, "There she is right now."

One of them jumped up and pushed my parka back off my head and said "Where's the gray hair? Must have been a woman wrote that."

Another said, "Yeah, it was a woman."

When I finally got a look at the paper, sure enough, the last paragraph said: Two years ago this slender, gray-eyed woman with the silver-sprinkled hair broke her back. Today she drives mechanical equipment weighing eight tons, and does most of the maintenance work herself. Who said something about a "will and a way?"

I took Fran's head off next time I saw her. Why did she have to call attention to my gray hairs? But the story she wrote which was spread across the front page was the cutest ever.

It started out with: "Chugging up the highway, twisting, turning, backing, climbing, came a jeep to Fairbanks last week.

"On the jeep were many red gasoline cans. In the jeep was a 110-volt 3,000-watt Kohler light plant, a 36-gallon gas tank, a husky pup and one woman.

"To the jeep was attached a 32-foot Liberty trailer with a heated floor, seven closets, a shower, kitchen, studio room with end tables and bridge lamps, a bedroom, chest of drawers, built-in cupboards, darkroom fully furnished with an enlarger and other photo equipment, a 40-gallon tank of water, refrigerator, electric steam radiator, an electric pump and a Persian kitten.

"One year ago on Labor Day, Iris Woolcock, free lance photographer, left her 200-acre farm in Vermont with Alaska in mind. A few detriments like a 4000-mile detour to swap trailers, several flats—which she changed—a natural and absorbing curiosity about places and people, and uncontrolable instinct to photograph everything, everywhere, caused her to progress slowly.

"But she got here.

"There were times she says when she met so many people coming back from Fairbanks—ones who had passed her going to the city—that she felt like moving picture running in reverse."

Then she went on telling of my past work, travels, etc. And then "Interested in everything from politics to root-cellars, vivacious, attractive Mrs. Woolcock lives a world citizen's life— home is where she hangs her hat (she should have said where I park my trailer), friends wherever there are people, pictures wherever there is light."

Guess that made up for the gray hair.

The soldiers started up the juke box. A lieutenant asked me to dance. A captain took me away from the lieutenant and whisked me out to the camp at Big Delta for dinner. A colonel took me away from the captain to the movies. Then I took things into my own hands and started working backwards. Captain Piteri was doing an excellent job of the recreational work at Big Delta. He said if I wanted the job of hostess I could have it with my choice of any camp in Alaska, very good salary and all expenses. That might have been a good way to stay there for awhile and save a bit of money. I sometimes regret not having taken it in order to learn some more about the north country, though my time might all have been spent listening to the lives and loves and problems of the soldiers and hearing how they all disliked military life in Alaska.

After I left Triangle I covered but a few miles when I stalled on a hill. Couldn't understand why until I got out to size up the situation. There was flat tire on the trailer. Again I thought about the signaling device to warn about trailer tires.

Before I even had my tools out a truck came by and out hopped three men who made short work of changing the wheel for me. While they were working at it another truck came along heading my way, parked front of me till I was ready to start, then hooked on and pulled me up over the hill. It would have been hard for me to make it without a good start from the bottom. This driver stayed near me the rest of the afternoon to make sure I didn't get into any more trouble, helped me find a good place to park for the night, and then before leaving, gave the jeep and the Kohler a once over and cleaned the sediment bowl on the Kohler.

I have a list of the names of a good many of the people who were so kind to me all along the highway. If I had all their names it would certainly add up to a considerable number. I just hope they all know how much I appreciate the things they did for me, their courtesy and their genuine friendliness.

Before I reached Tok the next afternoon, just as it was beginning to snow and I was hustling along over a long straight stretch (the only one in 1,600 miles), there was suddenly a terrific noise. It sounded as though the trailer had broken in two. With the brakes such as they were I couldn't stop for several hundred feet.

A wheel had come off the trailer. It happens to altogether too many trailers. It is invariably a left wheel — and why? Will they ever learn to build them as they do trucks and many cars and put LEFT hand lugs on the wheels on the LEFT side?

The wheel had rolled along with the trailer, remaining within the housing with the tire still intact. I was standing there looking at it when a familiar red bus drove up with a driver I had met and talked with many times. He studied the wheel and we both took it for granted that the bolts were all broken and lost.

I told him to give a message to Abe in Tok asking him to bring his traveling machine shop truck out to help me after he finished work that evening. I spent the rest of the afternoon in comfort in the trailer. Since I was on a slope, the oil stove wouldn't burn, but the old faithful Kohler kept all the electric radiators going so I was cozy and warm.

When Abe arrived he jacked up the trailer and found two of the wheel bolts rolling around in the hub cap. None of them had broken — they had just come out. Lots of snow had fallen by that time, and it was very dark of course, so we didn't have much hope of finding the other bolts which had obviously dropped along the road between the place I was stopped and the spot where the wheel came off. We found two. That gave me four to run on into Tok. Had I only gone to work at it myself I could have put the wheel on without waiting for help.

Earlier in the day I had smelled hot rubber. One of the spares, being heavy for the jeep tire carrier, had broken loose enough to rub against one of the rear jeep wheels so I had to take it off and give it a comfortable berth in the trailer until Abe could fix things up. And the other boys in the Tok maintenance camp were very helpful.

Next morning Patrolman Laird and his wife asked me to ride back to Verrick Bridge with them to photograph an accident. A couple had just bought a brand new car in Fairbanks and started for what was to be a swell vacation trip to the states. Trouble was they were trying to get there too fast and at the same time trying to do away with the large supply of liquor. For no good reason they lost control of the car, fortunately within sight and hearing of Mr. and Mrs. Elenes who run a lodge at the end of the bridge. They were whisked off to a hospital but it was doubtful whether the woman would recover.

26. A GRISLY MEAL

At Snag my old customs official friend, Frank Algar, had gone off for the weekend leaving the place in charge of a new man he had been training. Ned was so afraid of making a mistake he didn't dare let me by with all my outfit and paraphernalia. He thought Frank would be back next morning, but he wasn't.

I told him I didn't like to wait over any longer. Still he was worried stiff. All my cameras, film, machinery, guns, cat, etc.—he just didn't know what to do about all those things and couldn't seem to find rules and regulations covering anything like it.

I thought I remembered seeing where Frank had filed the papers I turned in when going north. These papers showed how the Canadian customs had listed things when I entered Canada from the south. I was lucky enough to find those papers and when Ned saw how they had let me by with it all down at Coutts he decided he'd take a chance on letting me go.

The snow was all off the road at Snag but the frost and ice on trees made the world look like a most beautiful fairyland. After leaving the customs office (with a gift of a sack of potatoes) I breezed along 102 miles to the nice parking spot where the trailer led in to the Burwash Creek mines. Familiarity with the road and the good parking places made things a bit easier on the way down.

Next day the dust was bad again and that merciless gravel gave me another flat. Never again over that road without the heavy bar or knobby tread tires which cannot pick up that confounded sharp gravel.

On reaching Kluane Lake, Game Warden Chambers and his wife said Annie Haydon was returning from her trial in Whitehorse that afternoon and that I really should meet her. She was the Indian woman who had killed her white husband and whose son I had met on the way up. There was a nice spot to park my trailer in front of Annie's house a few miles down around the lake. I pulled in just as she was arriving from the bus. Thinking she might not have much food in the house, I stepped across a lot of blood and brains on the threshold to offer her some cans of veal stew.

Within ten minutes we were bosom friends and I was invited for supper. She prepared a fine meal without having to open the cans. She had brought home a lot of fresh groceries, canned fruit, etc. from Whitehorse. I had to look at that threshold once in a while to make myself believe I was enjoying the hospitality of an honest-to-goodness murderess.

And then when her son came in saying he had just seen a big brown bear vanishing from sight around the mountain, Annie bemoaned the fact that the police had not yet given her gun back to her. She couldn't get along without her rifle. It was her 306 and her never-failing marksmanship that had kept the family supplied with their meat, furs and hides. And it was a quick shot from the 306 that dropped her husband on the threshold as he re-entered the house after one of their quarrels when he had cuffed her around and given her a couple of bad scratches on the wrist. She had had enough of such treatment.

A brand new car. A spoiled vacation trip. Too much snow, too much alcohol.

"I suppose you'll be much happier now without him," I said.

"Oh yes," she said, "I don't know why I ever put up with him for thirty years."

"He must have been pretty mean to you."

"He was mean," she said. "He knock me around and he all the time

talk mean. He think I know nothing. He think he only one ever know
anything. He never have no love, no kindness. When he was young, he
never had no family nor relatives. He didn't know what happy family
could be. He never had no upbringing. He just drug himself up."

"Now me," she went on, "I knew what it means to love family.
I had nice family. Lots of relations. I like go see my relations. He
never let me. He drag me off up here and marry me when I thirteen
years old."

The house they lived in was a good looking log cabin. The one huge
room inside had an arty atmosphere about it and almost made me think
I was in Greenwich Village. It had enormous old English stoves and
some rather interesting old furniture with some antique china and a lot
of nice pewter on the shelves. Books on mineralogy lined the shelves
around one corner. Some rugs and grass hung on the walls, and some
hung as partitions for the bedrooms, and, believe it or not, a bathroom
in one corner where a shower had been improvised with an overhead
barrel to hold rainwater or melting snow.

It seems the Haydons had bought the house from an Englishman
who had played around those parts prospecting and hunting.

Annie was loved by everyone who knew her, but Rube Chambers
said, "After all, it might have been well to give her a couple of years
just to keep too many women from thinking they might so readily
bump off their husbands." And Annie had enjoyed her three or four

Annie Haydon and
her son Eddie.
Husband's blood
and brains still
on the doorstep,
I was having
lunch with an
honest-to-
goodness
murderess!

weeks in jail while awaiting trial. She had been showered with gifts as she might have been had she been ill in a hospital.

But men are a dime a dozen up in that country.

Another woman killed a man with an axe. When the judge asked her why she did it, she said he backed his truck onto her clothesline and ran her nice white sheets into the mud after a hard day's wash.

She picked up the nearest thing handy which happened to be an axe and let fly with it. "Dismissed. Call the next case," said the judge.

Not far below where Annie Haydon lived there was an Indian cemetery unlike anything I have ever seen. The Indians build houses over the graves for spirits to live in. It looked like a hill covered with doll houses, all bright colors with gay curtains in the windows. If the family was too poor to build the house immediately a tent was pitched over the grave to give the soul shelter until the house could be built.

I wish I had stopped to see Mrs. MacIntosh on my way up, or could have visited her longer on my way down. She is one of the most attractive persons on the highway, and very much a part of it. A native of California, with a PhD from Columbia, she had married a retired mounty who had policed the Klondike during the gold rush and settled in the spot he liked best at Bear Creek. After his death in '38, no place else appealed to her as much as this home in the cold wilderness. So there she has continued to live alone, operating a little trading post. And she smiles now because the civilization from which she and her husband fled has been brought to her front door.

A compliment I shall treasure as long as I live was her invitation, extended after our very brief visit, for me to come and live with her. It thrilled me to have her say she felt I was one of her kind and that she was sure we could get along happily together. She must be in her seventies, and though her hair is snowy white, her beautiful, fresh, young face without a wrinkle, naturally pink cheeks and the bluest of all blue eyes make her seem not a day over forty-five. And I guess she keeps her lithe, graceful figure by hiring no help whatsoever in the job of getting up the enormous amount of wood she burns. And she refuses to get any supply worked up ahead.

She says the daily chore of chopping, sawing, splitting, hauling etc. forces her to get the amount of exercise she feels she needs each day. She has equipped her charming and immaculate house with modern plumbing. Having no electricity, she pumps water from a well under the house up into a supply tank upstairs from which it has enough pressure to supply the kitchen, bathroom and a large hot water tank heated by the kitchen stove.

Anyone any time can drop in and be cheerfully served a snack or a large meal. I wonder, though, when more and more tourists begin to flock up the highway, if it will become profitable or just tiresome.

Siebens Trans-American Adventures. A well-equipped outfit for real travel.

Weight and speed on gravel is murder on tires. The tires are apt to catch fire and on a tandem trailer burning tires can go unnoticed till far gone. Here the Juhnke family helps me change a burned up tire.

27. A RACE AGAINST THE COLD

Jack Whitlock certainly stood by his word that he was going to see to it I got back down that highway safely, and he was worried about my running into dangerous if not impossible snow and ice. I would not have taken any chances on dangerously icy hills and if things got too bad I would simply have waited until it was safer.

It might have taken me much longer to make the trip down if I had not been very lucky about the weather and ice and snow, and now that it was getting worse Jack was there, up and down the road, in front of me or in back of me, and usually right there in case I needed help. He had scooted up in a jeep and it sure came in handy. On some steep, snowy hills where I needed chains, the chains pulled my power down and I'd find Jack waiting to hook his jeep on in front of mine at the foot of any hills he was afraid I couldn't make on my own.

It was hard to predict. I'd make a few hard climbs on my own and then sometimes get stuck on an almost level spot. I was glad to have some help when it came to the countless times I had to put chains on and take them off. I found just one pair of light chains on the front wheels was the most helpful much of the time. This made it easier to steer straight where it was slippery and roughened up the ice just enough for the rear wheels to get more traction.

Then something happened to my fan. A blade started to crack off. I had it welded at Whitehorse but it didn't hold. It started hitting the radiator. Jack broke it entirely off. Don't ever try to drive with a fan with THREE blades. A few more revolutions and it would have wrecked the entire jeep. Then Jack took the opposite blade off and it worked.

Next evening, while parked at the Swift River Repeater Station where I had promised I'd stop on my way down, I had a wonderful evening.

There was some bad ice below Lower Post and I was really tired from the strain of driving when I finally reached Coal River. But it was fun seeing the repeater bunch there again and after a good moose meat dinner I gave them a show of Central American slides. I also let them see my little old farm in Vermont "dripping with hollyhocks and roses" as one of the newspaper reporters had described it after seeing the pictures on my trailer wall.

Next morning I was terribly disappointed to see it snowing hard. In spite of the snow I wanted to go and have a swim in the hot springs where the kids at the repeater station told of having fun swimming all winter. Getting dry and dressed in subzero weather was a trick and they said their hair would freeze in fantastic shapes. But they would build a big bonfire near the pool and have lots of fun. I thought pictures of swimming in the snow would have been well worth taking and I adore swimming in WARM water, but Jack was doing his darndest to get me to hustle down out of that country. He was trying to scare me about what hazardous road conditions I might meet if I didn't hurry. And I guess he also knew that I didn't realize how low the thermometer might drop at any minute.

I was putting in very short days of driving because the days were getting so short the sunsets were beginning to color the skies about three o'clock. I did NOT like the drive after dark, especially on steep hills and sharp curves. I got mad at Jack for insisting that I follow him up over Steamboat Mountain and meet him down at the other side of it AFTER DARK. I did it, but should NOT have done it. That was a nerve racking stretch of driving. Next morning I found a flat on the trailer and I thanked my lucky stars it hadn't gone the night before when rounding one of those steep sharp curves.

Swift River
Repeater
Station

28. FORT NELSON AND THE PROPHET OF TRUTCH

Just before I pulled into Fort Nelson what should I see passing me, heading north, but the twin to my trailer — a brand new thirty-three foot Liberty. It was being pulled by a new Hudson. I inquired about it at Fort Nelson and my friends in the garage there said it had stopped there for gas and an oil change. It was an army officer from Alaska with his wife and child, taking the trailer up to live in. The garage boys had asked him whether he thought he'd ever get there pulling a heavy trailer like that with a car. He said he'd had good luck so far and he thought luck and the grace of God would get him there. I told the boys I'd be willing to make a big wager that luck and the grace of God wouldn't be enough.

And it wasn't. Next thing I heard he was thanking God that his wife and child were still alive. He stalled and jackknifed on one of those icy hills a little farther up. The trailer broke loose and went crashing down over the mountain side. He took one look and drove on thanking his lucky stars that it did not take the car down with it. I guess no one has ever tried to go down to try to salvage an atom of either the trailer or its contents. And the last I heard of the officer he was still paying unhappily for a trailer home he didn't have.

An automatic electric attachment which would set trailer brakes when it tears loose from the car would probably have saved that trailer. Never another trailer trip for me without such an attachment.

At the Fort Nelson garage Bob Bartholet and Jack took a look over some of my mechanical equipment. When we examined the spark plugs in the Kohler everyone took his hat off to that machine for running at all. There were no points left in those plugs so they put in a new set.

The little village of Fort Nelson had to get its water from the airport. I rode over with Bob to get his tankload of water and then he filled my plumbing system. I made a good apple pie and invited him into dinner and he brought a lot of very interesting pictures of the early days of the highway construction to show me.

And I had other callers. I never stopped that trailer anywhere along the road now, or parked anywhere for overnight without at least one knock, and usually several, on the door. I didn't recall ever having seen some of my visitors, but they would refresh my memory by telling me how they had helped me change a tire or pulled me up a hill or, in the case of this young couple, the chap said he had filled my gas tanks in Fairbanks.

Sometimes it irked me to have tourists come to the door and brazenly say, "We'd like to see the inside of your trailer." They'd get a cold, "Sorry it's not on exhibition." The women were usually the curious ones who wanted to go through it. But there weren't many of that objectionable type and I cordially invited scores of scores of nice people I met to look through, knowing how interested they all were to see its insides.

I added to my stock of food by picking up some good apples from an upset apple cart I found beside the road. Some driver had tried to make a curve too fast and there was the wreckage of a large truckload of "Dependable Apples." The apples and their "Dependable" labels were scattered all over the landscape. I can't understand why the Canadian Army wasn't guarding those ruins to see to it that not a single apple was salvaged and consumed by any human being or animal in Canada.

About the same time, another truck overturned near the same place, Mile 207, just north of Trutch. It was a huge diesel operated by the Alaska Freight Lines and loaded with about 14 tons of assorted vegetables and fruits bound for Fairbanks. The cab was nearly demolished, but the occupants escaped serious injury.

H. Noakes of Trutch reported that immediately after the accident, C.N.T. wires were burning with messages resulting in orders being issued that a guard was to be placed at once on the truck to see that no one touched any of the load under penalty of nothing short of death. Huge chains, bars, and locks were rushed from a nearby maintenance camp at Trutch. Then these were placed all around the van containing the precious load and tightened and secured with locks.

The load of choice foods was left to spoil, while, as Mr. Noakes says, "daily we are told by radio and press about the millions of people who are starving in Europe many of whom will die this winter through malnutrition. Yet the same government that pleads with you and me to give — give to this most worthy cause so their self-made red-tape laws can be enforced—encouraged the criminal waste of so much food.

"Through a simple order it could have been transferred via another truck and turned over to that most worthy cause known as C.A.R.E. who would have distributed it thereby relieving suffering among the needy.

"Instead, this food was left just where it landed after the accident for about a week, after which a bright, new, shiny car arrived at the scene operated by a police officer of the B.C. police department who was all dressed in a spotless khaki uniform with nice shiny buttons and boots. He was accompanied by a similarly dressed Canadian customs officer who wore a tailor-made dark uniform with gold buttons and a cap to match, trimmed with gold braid. Another person was with the officers, dressed in ordinary civilian clothes with no trimmings, evidently a vegetarian by his appearance, and possibly the chief mourner, because we heard a cremation was about to take place."

"Oh yes," went on Mr. Noakes, "gasoline was conveyed to the spot where the load of vegetables and fruit lay, and there a most solemn ceremony took place in which the entire 14 tons of good food was cremated, the while the faint strains of Beethoven's funeral march could be heard away in the distance, as Trutch was enveloped for hours by dense clouds of smoke which reeked with the odors of cooked, frozen vegetables and fruits.

"What does all this mean? It means that considerable monies of the simple taxpayer were squandered in the waste of gasoline, automobile usage, officers' expenses, not to mention the waste of time in which their services could have been put to better use. All so that several tons of the finest food stuffs could be burnt, and this at a time when other human beings are dying because they have no food upon which to exist. All of which makes one realize just what a wonderful country we are privileged to live in, and what a wonderful system is our democracy. If we had the rare gift, even as minute as the proverbial grain of mustard seed with which our Robert Service was blessed, we could make his famous poem 'The Cremation of Sam McGee' read like a nursery rhyme."

The aluminum van came through the fire in which its contents were destroyed and appeared in good enough shape to be put to profitable use in the freighting business. There was great need for trucks in Canada — demand constantly exceeding supply. A friend of Mr. Noakes who was in the freighting business looked it over and wanted very much to make use of it. He communicated with the authorities and was advised that "this van is not of this country and orders have been issued by which it shall be crushed into the ground by means of passing over it a huge bulldozer." The friend remarked, "Following which it most assuredly will then become very definitely of this country. Strange goings on, don't you agree?"

This Mr. Noakes was has courage enough to express his opinions on such subjects in his column, News 'n Nonsense from Trutch, in the weekly *Alaska Highway News*, has been suddenly and rudely evicted from his gas station, office, lunch room and quarters at Trutch which he had leased from the Canadian Army. I wonder why —or do I?

I should like to hear his opinion on the destroying and burying of that vast amount of valuable road equipment, machinery and tools. I do have his opinion aptly expressed on how the maintenance of the road is being carried on with the decrepit, broken-down bits of inadequate road equipment which are all the Canadians have and with which they are doing a woefully insufficient job.

Noakes says, "Now we know why in Dawson Creek they erect a sign in the center of the main intersection, which sign reads: Mile 0 The

Alaska Highway.

"Riding into Dawson Creek from the Alaska Highway it should be quite plain to everyone, as it is to us, that after sinking into, plowing out of, and straddling across the million-and-a-half deep holes which comprise the entire road surface in that piece of highway immediately entering Dawson Creek, that the 0 referred to in the sign is put there to warn motorists about the holes ahead. After all it matters not which way you choose to go from the sign, there are holes a-plenty awaiting to test your skill as a driver, your auto's durability, your patience, and your physical endurance."

He goes on with, "Driving into, through and out of both Fort St. John and Dawson Creek this past weekend made one appreciate more than ever the skills and modern achievements of our present day automotive engineers who are able to manufacture a piece of equipment which will withstand such a terrific beating and emerge still a going concern — no more do we wonder why there are to be found in Fort St. John and Dawson Creek so many garages and subsidiary places who derive their entire livelihood from the weaknesses and defects of the automobile.

"If it is funds the corporations of Fort St. John and Dawson Creek require in order to improve their roads all they have to do is to notify two or three of the leading automobile manufacturers that they have for immediate rental the finest automobile proving grounds on the North American continent. NEVER could the designers of automobile proving grounds ever conceive of such rugged terrain as one can find in and around Fort St. John and Dawson Creek. Local folks in and around these two bump-impregnated areas are the innocent victims of a new form of disease designated 'Buttock Bumpingitis'. Some American big game hunters remarked that a couple of days riding around these parts was sure good for getting one in shape for the saddle."

Then he rubs it in further by saying, "What puzzles us is how local Dawson Creek merchants can go on year in and year out sympathizing with the poor tourist or traveler just fresh in from that mile after mile of mud baths located between Edmonton and Dawson Creek, patting him on the back, giving him a line of sales malarkey found only south of the mighty Peace, well knowing that after leaving their store he will find himself driving over a piece of highway, the equivalent of No-Man's Land filled with mine craters, when all the time he thinks he is on the Alaska Highway, the highway the Dawson Creek merchant uses as his source of tourist business and sales ballyhoo. Shame on somebody.

"Now they have a golf course in Dawson Creek— a sheer waste of good money. Why should anyone wish to waste money on green fees when all you have to do to get a hole-in-one is to simply drive into Dawson Creek from any direction, anytime. FORE."

When the highway was turned over to the Canadians there were

some small portions of it which did not yet have the final covering of
gravel and it was supposed that Canada would take hold where the U.S.
left off and finish these sections. But no, they are just leaving it with its
murderous surface of large stones which get pushed from side to side and
work havoc with tires and cars.

"When asked WHY they don't do something about it—the same old
answer—lack of men, money and machines. Now about all those
valuable machines, replacement parts and other very useful equipment
buried in those trenches? Just WHO are the men in Canada who see to
it that such laws are made to keep the people in Canada from having
better roads, better machinery, more refrigerators, and a higher standard of living?"

"Our economy can't afford such extravagances," said the gentlemen
in the customs office.

Since there are fewer people in Canada and since their economy does
not seem quite as complex as ours, I think it would be fairly easy to find
the handful of people who are working to keep Canada a backward
country. These few have been making lots of money for a good many
months. Their business is big enough and good enough—they wish to
keep things just as they are.

Should they spread out and enlarge their own industries, railroads
and factories, and should they build roads and open up large sections of
rich resources, things might get too big to keep well in hand. They are
making sure things don't grow too fast—they might lose control. And
they don't want an American made machine used in maintaining the
road. That would mean the loss of a sale when and if their factory ever
gets around to making such a machine. Oh yes, the laws are made to
protect Canadian business and MUST be enforced.

If knocking down the border between our two countries could only be
put to a vote, the people in the United States would surely vote
unanimously for it. All the people in Canada would vote for it—
EXCEPT those few who are feathering their beds with their monopolies
and have money enough to keep their politicians happy—the ones whose
votes would be counted.

It would be hard to find a single vote against the consolidation of the
two countries in the western sections. In the east there would be only the
aforesaid few against it. And in the east there is a rather big piece of
business in which the two countries have mutual interest — the St.
Lawrence Waterway Power Project. The U.S. has lagged behind in
upholding its end of that agreement.

When I pulled into Trutch on November 11th, there was no evidence
of its being the holiday we call Armistice Day. His Honor, the mayor, was
talking to an old timer about the recent big game hunting season. They
were trying to find a reason for the reported shortage of game and the old

timer finally 'lowed as how it was largely due to the animals being slightly indisposed, suffering from cut feet caused by crossing the Alaska Highway where they step on large pieces of broken bottle glass lying in the roadway.

This applied especially to the moose and caribou who have large feet. He said there was one moose that was injured seriously but would have escaped the hunter who shot him, had he not been unable to do so by reason of a badly cut foot. He was located lying in the dense brush by the hunter, nursing his foot and singing, "Roll Out the Barrel."

"So you see why the boys failed to get their moose this year."

Then there followed a lengthy discussion as to how the glass got into the middle of the highway, the concensus of opinion being that the imbibers of some potent stuff be able to make the ditch bordering the highway in throwing an empty bottle. Was it just hellishness to drop the empties right in the middle of the road? Whatever it was, only very unsportsmanlike, inconsiderate people could be so unconcerned about the safety of others who ply the Alaska Highway and whose lives are endangered through tire blow-outs, especially the folks from the U.S.A. who drive late model high-powered cars and are used to driving along paved highways where speed is the order of the day. Then they decided the beer drinkers were a very selfish lot. "To date we have never yet found a bottle full of beer among the hundreds discarded."

Noakes wrote of meeting a moose that hunting season. In his column he told about driving to town the middle of October:

"Arriving at Mile 31 which is almost the summit of the Peace River hill in the fast growing darkness, and with our parking lights on, we saw what appeared to be a man standing in the roadway awaiting a ride into town. This was a pleasurable sight and we made ready to pick him up by moving our baggage so as to make room, thinking the while how nice it was going to be to be able to share with him during the intervening miles, our sincere feelings about this great land we were both living off."

"It was not until we had approached to within about one hundred yards of the object we had thought to be a hitchhiker, that we observed it to be a full grown bull moose. It was standing square in the center of the road, facing us. Visibility was very poor. We had hated to put on our bright lights as we were loathe to spoil a perfect evening, and with no other traffic on the highway, it seemed criminal to do so.

Upon stopping our truck, not wishing to suffer a deflated radiator, we switched on our bright lights, alternating them once or twice with the aid of the dimmer switch, hoping to scare the moose off the road so that we might pass. Instead of offering to move, the beast lowered his head and commenced to proceed towards us with a definite businesslike approach. This movement on his part caused us to gear into reverse and back up.

I gave these kids a talk and showed them pictures of the other end of their great highway down through Central America.

"Next we tried our horn (a wheezy, congested pip-squeak affair). This had the effect of making the moose raise his head and shake it. It was then we got a good look at the animal. What a specimen. It was huge, with a bulk of a body, and puffed neck which would make a full grown Percheron stud's neck look like a Shetland pony's. His antlers were the largest we have ever seen on a live moose. Apparently our horn must have given him the impression it was coming from an asthmatic cow moose because he commenced to show far less aggressiveness after each blast, or peep of the horn.

"Next we tried racing up the motor, but this did not even phase him as he stood resolutely right in the middle of the road. Following a full five minutes in which we tried all things already mentioned, coupled with dismounting and throwing stones at the moose, he finally, but very reluctantly, ambled off into the low bush on the west side of the highway.

"Here he stood defiantly looking at us, as we slowly passed by not more than 50 yards away. A perfect shot, and us with a nice new game license, moose tag and rifle at home in Trutch, where one may have to walk days before even coming across a moose track."

"However," continues the Prophet of Trutch, "this incident merely served to further our already firm conviction that this Peace River country is indeed a paradise in which to live, where abound all the things necessary for the survival of mankind, such as wild and cultivated food, birds, fish and animal life for the taking. Surely not one of us living in the Peace River country permitted this past Thanksgiving to pass without at least one sincere prayer to the Almighty for His bountiful gifts of nature over this past year."

29. MURDERS, FULLER BRUSHES, AND OTHER TALES

As the road comes on down from Trutch there are points from which one can see it as it winds its way over the mountains for miles and miles ahead and behind.

Not far from Trutch was the place where Gustave Weigner had shot John McComas and where, while I was on my way up, the body had been found with the arms chewed off. After Weigner was caught, having run off with McComas' money and daughter, he was sentenced to two years at hard labor for the killing. He said he shot McComas by mistake when aiming at a squirrel.

Asking his worship, the Mayor of Trutch, B.C. what he thought of this, he said, "Well, I wouldn't care to be in his (Weigner's) shoes. Everyone traveling the highway must see that sign in a tree situated at or near Mile 70 which reads in part: 'No person shall shoot any firearm within a mile of the highway on either side from here on.' Then you must remember that at the time of the shooting of his companion, John McComas, the game season had not yet opened, and if you recall, he said he was shooting at squirrels. So you see there can be no excuse for him in so far as the B.C. Game Department is concerned, as after all, he wore glasses. So therefore he could not have missed seeing the sign. Maybe the Game Department will give this squirrel-minded moron what's coming to him."

Then the mayor added, "Confidentially speaking, it has been said that some individuals along the highway who are not what might be called hail fellows well met, have been observed in town of late and it is alleged they are seeking additional insurance since the Weigner affair. Who knows, maybe such a precedent set by the courts in Victoria in this case, could cause someone else to believe it to be expedient to try to get himself a squirrel, more especially now that the season is open officially. As you all know, accidents will occur. Besides it's not nice to be eaten up by wolves and bears and things, is it?"

My son was worried about my safety in the northern wilds and sent me a clipping marked BE CAREFUL. The clipping from the *Nation* said, "Alaska has vast open spaces but no wilderness police force to compare with the Royal Mounted of Canada. A criminal recently apprehended in

Alaska confessed to six murders. Territorial law enforcement officials did not even know his victims were missing. A federal judge told me that prospectors and trappers disappear in 'the bush' and no one ever looks for them. 'Not only are criminals uncaught generally in Alaska, but I am convinced there is no real knowledge of what crimes are committed.'"

I wasn't worried. No one could bump me off and get away very far with my extremely unusual and conspicuous outfit. And strangers coming across a trailer parked away off in some remote spot wouldn't know how many people or how many guns were inside it. Those who knew me and knew I was traveling alone probably knew also that I had guns.

Anyway, what's the use of being afraid? There's as much danger on the top floor of a crowded New York apartment building. My mother was the victim of a horrible attempt at murder by a robber who climbed through her bathroom window assisting himself by a rope tied to the roof. So if you're going to be afraid you might as well be afraid all the time no matter where you are.

And, after all, the Alaska Highway is not so remote that, believe it or not, the Fuller Brush Man has not found it. From Mr. Noakes again I quote: "Yes sir, today we've seen everything. Right on a doorstep. (Oh yes we have them in Trutch — to our American cousins we mean stoop). We saw a lady very minutely examining samples of the very dinkiest brushes. And whose brushes do you think they were? The Fuller Brush Man's. He had brushes for this and that, even one to brush up on. All of course included the d—d three percent tax. We suppose that's what made the bristles stand up."

Pulling into the grounds of Mason Creek Lodge to park for the night, and going in to the lunch counter for a meal, I became engaged in conversation with a truck driver who had made a trip down from Fairbanks to get a large truckload of supplies for an Alaskan market.

He went around ordering stuff from various departments in one of the big wholesale houses in Seattle, added up the quoted prices and went to the office to settle up while the stuff was being loaded into his truck. By that time someone had discovered it was to be taken to Alaska and excitedly called this information over the partial partition of the private office where the driver was about to pay the bill. The company official with whom he as dealing immediately scratched out the figures and informed the driver that it would total considerably more since it was going to Alaska. The driver was faced with the choice of paying the very much higher bill or leaving the supplies behind. He inquired at some of the other wholesale depots and found it to be the same racket everywhere in Seattle — a disgusting imposition carried on obviously by those who are carrying on their greedy monopolies and trying to keep their stranglehold on Alaska.

   It was this truck driver's first round trip on the highway and when he was asking me for some suggestions as to good stopovers and eating places along the road, Jack Whitlock pushed his way between us, straddling the bench with his back to me, cutting me off abruptly and completely from any further conversation with the truck driver.

   This I did not consider very good manners on the part of an Oxford graduate born of a titled English family. Lots of things I couldn't understand about Jack. He was so very sweet and kind in many ways and so rude and thoughtless in others. Or wasn't he thoughtless? Did he think ladies shouldn't talk with truck drivers, or did he think a woman he happened to fancy shouldn't talk to other men?

   Jack sure was trying to rush things. I had met him just a few days before leaving Grande Prairie, had enjoyed fishing with him, and he had been so kind and helpful in chasing up the highway with the piece of starter mechanism, and now again driving away off up the highway to be of assistance in many places with the ice and snow and more difficult going and hill climbing, BUT, this time when I met him on the highway he had with him two rings. One a lovely old cameo from his family keepsakes, and the other—a diamond.

   "Hold on," said I, thinking to myself that the speed with which these men of the north seem to work might please some impulsive women, but not me.

   In Fort St. John I broke an axle and was glad for an excuse to stay there for awhile. Jack hustled onto Grande Prairie and sent one up by air so it reached the Fort St. John garage next day.

Homemade road signs near Watson Lake.

30. FORT ST. JOHN

Fort St. John boasts a population of about a thousand. From what I saw of it, that figure must include the airport and considerable outlying territory.

It is a town of strange contrasts. While looking at something ultra-modern you simultaneously see a bit of the most primitive type of life. There is the fine airport with planes of all types, clippers, jets, packets and Piper Cubs zooming in and out any and all hours of the day or night with the field always kept clear of snow for them.

But on roads half a mile from the airport children die in wagon races with death. Georgina Murray said, "Of course motor cars are fine—IF we could get them, and IF we could get enough snow plows to keep frontier roads clear."

Georgina says that the people have money and they spend it. She says they buy good books, good soap and good food. But that the Canadian economy I heard so much about keeps them from having automobiles and many other things they could use and enjoy. The number of cars they are allowed to import is very limited. One dealer told me he could sell thirty times as many as his quota allows him to import from the states. And by the time a car gets there the Canadian customer has to pay about twice as much as we pay for the same car. The duty is so terribly high, and then of course the transportation helps run up the price.

The Hudson's Bay Trading Post in Fort St. John didn't like being called a trading post. It was a very modern store with a toyland, a shoe department, fluorescent lights and smocked clerks. Georgina said it was getting to look more and more like an escalator was just around the corner. But in the manager's office Mr. Campbell was sitting behind a huge pile of fox pelts with mink, marten, lynx, and other furs heaped in every corner.

The trappers are known as men of silence. They have little to say even when they make their rare trips to town. They're just so used to being off in the wilds alone, talking seems to tire them.

There's the story I heard of the three old sourdoughs working their traplines in Alaska and living together in one cabin. After a couple of months of silence one morning at breakfast one of them said, "Saw a horse on the hill." Next morning the second said, "I didn't see no horse on the hill." The third got up saying, "I'm leaving. Can't stand this incessant wrangling."

Most people in Fort St. John buy their water by the barrel —.75¢. The waterman has quite a time delivering the water in the winter. He has to haul it from Charlie Lake, six miles away. The sleigh has a stove with the stack sticking up through the middle of the tank to keep at least some of the water from freezing until it can be dumped into the barrels at the kitchen doors. It worried him a bit when I got water from him because he couldn't tell just how much I was getting. Instead of carrying it and dumping from his pails, I made the job easier for him by handing him a hose to put into his tank, turning a couple of valves and letting my little electric pump draw it into my tank. He had to guess at the amount I was getting by watching the level in his tank.

They say he was a sight in really cold weather with his sleigh bells and pails jingling up the street and icicles dangling from everything including his elbows and mustache.

In contrast to the great fleets of trucks and traffic speeding up and down the Alaska Highway, are the horse drawn cabooses in which the families from the neighboring farms come into town to shop or go to church. The caboose is a cabin built on a sleigh with windows and a stove inside. Smoke pours out of the chimney as they drive along. I felt a kinship with them—as though they were distant cousins of my trailer.

Every time I went to the post office in Fort St. John I met Europeans there who could sparsely speak English and who were sending something to Europe. Georgina said many of these people left Europe by the underground in 1939 and came to Canada to join their armies. Now they were working hard here to keep their own families and at the same time, contributed to help the bitter plight of mothers, fathers, sisters and brothers in Europe. Georgina said, "I've read some of the letters that ask for help and they are indeed enough to cast a shadow over the heartiest of men."

The previous summer a couple of business girls from Detroit were heading up the Alaska Highway with a car and small trailer on a vacation trip. Helen Cole, formerly with the Ford Motor Company, got no further than Fort St. John. One of those nice bachelors from Baldonnel happened to be in town the day the girls arrived. Six weeks later Helen was married to him and living in his one room log cabin on his homestead ranch. How as wonderful a fellow as Royal Snapp had escaped being grabbed up long before was a wonder. Every free and unattached girl and every mother who had a daughter knew without a doubt that he'd make a perfect husband but it took Helen's executive training and ability or just the fact that she was one of the swellest gals in the world to land him.

Helen and Royal had a free and unattached friend they wanted me to meet out at Hudson's Hope. Sorry I didn't feel I should take time to go out there for a visit at the attractive hunting and fishing resort I heard this chap was building up. I had heard it talked up as THE place to go. Driving out a ways on that road I found a newly-constructed fine wide highway.

There was considerable activity in the coal mines beyond Hudson's Hope. The great patches of rusty red streaking down the walls of some of the cuts where the road wound around the mountains looked as though there must be iron deposits.

Such a fine road leading out there to the southwest of Fort St. John either meant that the resources they found were well worth going after, or, in the eternal squabble as to where the main road should eventually lead from the Peace River country to link up with the west coast, it might be that this section thought it could get the jump on the other proposed, and already started, routes.

It was really a lucky accident that caused the rear axle of my jeep to break as I was rounding a street corner in Fort St. John. I thought it was a deep hole in the street which caught the left rear wheel just right, but maybe it was about to go. In fact when they got the pieces out in Dave's Garage it looked as though it had started to crack a long ways back. But you'll have to hand it to the jeep for being able to continue on its way with only the front axle in working order. I hated to try to pull the trailer up the hill and around the block but when a truck came from the garage to tow me it couldn't budge me—its hind wheels just spun. So I started up the jeep and the front drive carried me right to where I wanted to park for my stay in the town.

And I'm certainly glad to have had that stay which I could have missed had the axle not broken. That seemed to be the way it was every time I suffered some delay for mechanical repairs. After things were fixed I usually had become so interested in the place that I was very loathe to get myself out and on my way again.

Pulling down the highway late the afternoon of November 20th, darkness, overtook me at Mile 20. It was tricky business crossing the Peace River Bridge that afternoon.

When I came to where I expected to be catching sight of the bridge any minute I thought a lake or an extremely wide river lay in the valley ahead of me. It looked smooth and white, like ice covered with snow. And no bridge could I see. I went down, down that steep long hill toward the river and finally the road went right smack into it — only it wasn't the river—it was the densest blanket of fog I had ever seen. It completely covered the river, bridge, road, oncoming traffic— everything. I edged over to what I hoped was the right side of the road, got out to feel around with my feet to make sure it was the side of the road and then got back in the jeep and sat there for a while with the lights all on. I heard a few big trucks inching their way up the hill toward me but couldn't see their lights till they were within a very few feet.

When I saw some lights right behind the trailer I walked back and found a car with a man who said he thought he knew the road well enough to find the bridge. He asked if I wanted to follow him. We stopped on the approach to the bridge. There was a weird light ahead which we couldn't figure out. The man went ahead with his car. I followed a ways on foot and he walked back to tell me it was a crew of men working at the west pier of the bridge and that they would hold back any traffic from the opposite direction until we reached them. It was like being suspended in space to be able to see no road, no bridge railing, nothing but a dim little light waving in the distance.

The fog at the east end wasn't so bad and I came out of it a few hundred yards beyond the bridge.

I pulled into the driveway of the maintenance camp at Mile 20, called the Kiskatinaw Camp. Then I knocked on the door of one of the usual type of barrack buildings to ask permission to park there for the night. There was the usual surprise of finding it fixed up as a very attractive home inside. It was the home of the road crew superintendent.

Mr. and Mrs. Wright invited me in and suggested that I attend the weekly movie with them that evening. I went back to my trailer to spruce up and when I rejoined them they were searching a top shelf finally coming out with a coffee pot. Then they began hunting in the back corners for the wherewithal to make the coffee. As in every such case, they were delighted to hear me say, "Oh please don't make coffee for me, I hate the stuff, but I love tea."

In dozens of the Canadian homes I visited they would immediately think, "Oh, an American—we must make her some coffee!" And then they would be so relieved and pleased to find that I preferred their tea.

While enjoying the tea and cake the cute little blond school teacher, Phyllis Boulanger (who surely won't last long up there) came in to say there would be no movie. But they were all planning to go to the dance at Sunrise Valley and would hear of nothing but that I would go with them. So we all piled into a very chilly truck and drove a few miles to that very charmingly-named settlement where the dance was being held in the school house.

After perching on one of the desks piled along side the room to watch the dancing, Mrs. Cooper, who had joined our party from Farmington, called my attention to a tall dark young man in a brown suede jacket leaning against the pillar near the entrance watching the dance floor with half open eyes.

"He looks drunk," she said.

"He's either sleepy or very bored," said I. "He may have had too much to drink, and it is warm in here. He's good looking—very interesting face."

"I'm sure he's terribly drunk," insisted Mrs. Cooper.

I promptly forgot about him and continued to be interested in watching the dancing and the auctioning off of the box lunches which took place soon after we arrived.

When the dancing resumed I noticed a figure standing in front of me. My eyes followed up past the brown suede jacket to the still half closed big brown eyes.

"Would you care to dance?"

I thought to myself, "I'll try almost anything once—this may prove to be a horribly difficult situation to handle if I start dancing with him and can't hold him up."

I climbed down off the desk and didn't have a chance to think any further. I found myself in the arms of one of the most wonderful partners I ever had the good fortune to dance with. I have been spoiled by having gone along through my life meeting some of the very finest of dancers— a Swedish artist who was absolutely tops, a Russian who danced as only the finest of the Russian dancers can dance, some of Arthur Murray's best pupils, and Jimmy Harris who used to take me to Harlem.

I was in seventh heaven dancing with this man. There were a few good waltzes, a rumba, but most of the music was the very peppy sort which the jitterbugs enjoy. I love strenuous dancing and I got my fill of it for four solid hours—though I could have stood more. I found myself doing things with him I'd never done before. He'd whirl me away from him and grab me back—almost apache stuff—maybe it was, or maybe it was only jitterbug. I was glad I had worn a full pleated skirt. My only concern was keeping my shoes on. (Contrary to some women's opinions, if you are continuously wearing soft flat soles, moccasins or big loose boots, your feet do not become larger. They seem to grow smaller. Every time I go back to city or dress shoes they seem a size or two larger than they should be.) In one kick I lost a shoe but was able to retrieve it pronto.

There were only a couple of intermissions during those four hours. When my partner asked me whether I'd care to go out to his truck for a bottle of beer I declined. Thought that might hurt his feelings but he was back at the first beat of the music again. The next intermission, I was so warm and so terribly thirsty it was one of the rare times in my life when I thought a drink of beer would really taste good. I was also curious to find out a bit more about my partner. He was a perfect gentlemen, quiet—neither of us said much. I can't understand now why I didn't even find out his name. I did ask what he was doing in that part of the country. "Building the new school house at Dawson Creek," he said. I guess I was just too out of breath to ask any more questions.

Toward the end of the dance the good looking blond gentlemen teacher of the school cut in several times. My languid-eyed partner let him have a few steps each time, but not many before he cut back in himself.

The dance ended with Home Sweet Home at 4:00 a.m.

When I got back to the trailer—Jack was there.

"You MUST hurry down out of this country before the roads become more dangerous or absolutely impassable. I won't rest till I get you to Grande Prairie where you'll be safe if the weather takes a turn for the worse."

I didn't see how the roads could become impassable for long, although I'll admit there was the bad stretch between Dawson Creek and Grande Prairie and I knew they were very negligent about plowing that section. In fact they didn't plow at all, but there was constant traffic which kept it open, even though there was but one set of ruts down the middle. I discovered when I got there that even though there had not been very much snow, I had to keep the chains on in order to be able to pull out to the side when passing.

That is a terrible stretch of road at any and all times—an absolute disgrace. You'd think, in all these years since the United States built that marvelous stretch of road from Dawson Creek to Fairbanks, the Canadian government would be frightfully ashamed of themselves and be unable to find any excuse for not having built a good piece of road over those few hundred miles from Edmonton to Dawson Creek.

Again, I say, KNOCK DOWN THE BORDER. We are all exactly the same kind of people, except that I don't think there are quite as many crooks and gangsters in Canada. The residents up there are smart enough to protect themselves against the bad elements which might find their way up among them. And those fine people up there certainly deserve any and all the benefits they might derive from a consolidation of our countries.

Maybe Howard Scott is right. He and his technocrats feel there can be no survival for the Western Hemisphere unless it consolidates—and quick. He says there is nothing else for us to do with the consolidation he sees as inevitable in Europe and Asia.

Regardless of what happens I just think anyone is a fool who cannot see what tremendous benefit it would be to us all if Canada and the U.S. were one.

31. GRAND PRAIRIE AT -40

The trailer began to act peculiarly as I neared Grande Prairie. Jack and his son Don were following me and couldn't seem to find what was wrong. When I got there and parked in back of the Whitlock establishment in a sheltered spot, and hooked up to their electricity, we found a rear axle had broken loose and slid back on one side. With the thermometer then at 40 below zero, no one wanted to crawl under the trailer and work on the cold metal. There was no place in the whole town big enough to get the trailer in under cover. It didn't go above 40 below for about three weeks. Then in a mild spell of 25 below Jack, undertook the difficult job of putting the trailer carriage in good order. He also gave the Kohler and jeep motors a complete overhauling and cleaning. No one could say Jack didn't enjoy work.

In his spare time he rebuilt a jeep station wagon in which he said he planned to visit the states. Jack insisted that if only I knew him well enough he felt pretty sure I'd decide that he could be a very useful companion. When I told him his part of the country was too cold to suit me he said he had a hunch he'd like Vermont pretty well. When I described my little old farm to him he said he thought it sounded ideal. "Always did like to putter around at fixing up a place," he said.

"Well, my farm certainly could do with a lot of fixing—always something to do around the place," I said. I told him it would please me to have him see it and visit me there and meet my friends and get acquainted with the states. Then I got scared when it looked as though he were packing up and planning to leave Grande Prairie for good.

"Hold on," again I said. "How do you know you'll like it down there?" Now don't go burning your bridges behind you. You seem to be so sure that you and I are going to be taking up life together. I'm not going to say I don't think there is any possible chance —I'm not absolutely sure. I would have to see you in my own home territory to make up my mind for a certainty. If you should fit into my old surroundings there among the things and the people who mean so much to m —there might be a chance. But it is a big gamble on your part. I don't want you to say I urged you to take the trip—it's all up to you."

He thought all that over seriously for a while and then announced that he would take the trip. Again I warned him to be sure he wanted to travel all those miles for the sake of having the trip and seeing the country — NOT just because of ME. He said yes, that was okay with him and he could attend to considerable business in the states, especially around Detroit and Toledo and where I planned to take the trailer back. Upon Mr. Spencer's invitation, the Liberty factory was going to rebuild it with many of the changes and improvements my "proving-ground" trip has shown necessary.

Jack said it would be impossible for him to negotiate such a trip under the Canadian restrictions allowing no one to take more than $150 down into the states. We therefore arranged that he should pay all my bills while I was in Grande Prairie and that I should use some of his Canadian money to travel from there on down through Canada and repay it all to him in American money after he got down into the states. All of which just goes to show how people will find ways of breaking laws or of wangling ways whereby they can get around the unreasonable restrictions imposed by that border line.

I cannot say I enjoyed that stay in Grande Prairie . I was warm and comfortable in my trailer, but the town was horribly unattractive in winter. I was glad my windows were completely frosted over most of the time because it gave me the blues every time I looked out. I became homesick for lovely Vermont, or the prairie sheep ranch in Montana, or anyplace but this hideous town. It was too cold to see much of the few very nice friends I had there — no one went out any more than necessary. I saw a couple of very good movies but almost died walking those few blocks. The cold air hurt my nose and throat and nearly choked me.

Jack kept telling me it was a good thing I wasn't still poking along down the highway. I don't see how it could have been much worse, and I would have had some better scenery to be looking at. But, I guess he really was right in that it would have been more difficult to keep the water pipes in the trailer from freezing, especially when driving, even with the electric heaters going all the time. And it was hard enough to keep motors from freezing up unmercifully.

It would probably have been necessary to keep the jeep and the Kohler both running constantly day and night. I had an electric heater installed in the jeep. It was a gadget they use a lot in the north country to keep the anti-freeze solution hot, but even with loads of alcohol in the gas, the fuel lines, pump, etc. were all apt to freeze. When people went to shop or to the movies or any place where the car had to stand outside, they usually left the motor running. Sometimes you could hardly see to drive down Main Street with all the clouds of white steamy exhaust from the lines of cars on both sides.

Georgina Murray said, "Idling motors on a cold night in St. John alone would contribute to an oil company's dividend at Christmas."

I spent most of my evenings in Grande Prairie printing pictures. I was bitterly disappointed in much of the work done with my Medalist. I had noticed some very poor shots, especially those done with flash, among some of the earlier pictures I made with it. I thought the fault must be with me, not the camera. Now I realized it was failing me miserably. So many of the shots I had taken of the activities of the interesting people up and down the highway and in Alaska — the ones I wanted most were not good enough to use for reproduction. That fact, together with what happened to some of my negatives in Fairbanks, made my photographic accomplishments on this trip look rather sad.

If the Medalist had not worked properly any of the time it would have been a help and I would have resorted to the use of the Speed Graphic and Leica entirely. Then I could have forgotton I had ever thrown something over four hundred dollars into the Medalist and its accessories thinking it would be the perfect camera for all the quick shooting I wanted to do. People are apt to get scared when they see a big Speed Graphic pointed at them. And I was using the Leica merely to get some Kodachrome slides for my own amusement.

I could have done much better on this trip had I confined myself to the use of two Leicas as I had done on my trips through Central America. I kept one loaded with color and one with black and white and brought back plenty of work good enough for any purpose. But this time I wanted to do much better and bring back black and whites to fill requests for higher standards in book and magazine illustration.

I tried to get a Roleiflex but they were almost impossible to find at the time. Had heard the Medalist #I was found unreliable when used by the Navy men for whom it was first designed during the war, but I believed all the Eastman Company said about ironing out all the bugs in the Medalist II. I thought at SUCH a price it certainly should be good. Just another example of what a dope I can be. No one else would have been foolish enough to start on such a trip without giving a new camera a more thorough tryout. However, its faults did not show up at first. Then it grew steadily worse. I did not want to be around Grande Prairie for Christmas when the friends I had there would be having family get togethers and feel they ought to include me, so I pulled out the 24th.

There were stretches of snowy and icy road, then clear stretches, but whenever I took off my chains I was sure to have to put them back on again in a few miles. Jack knew I'd have a time crossing the Smoky River on the ice. There was a tractor there to give people a hoist up over the terribly steep rocky bank, but Jack dashed out with a jeep and overtook me just as I approached the river. It was just about all both jeeps could do to pull up that horribly rough steep bank. And there were the periods in spring and fall when nothing could cross after the ferry could no longer run and the ice was not yet strong enough to drive across.

All the snow made it hard to find places to pull off the road to park.

Jack had said I'd find a cleared driveway and parking space at the Hudson's Bay store at Calais, near Sturgeon Lake. When I went in to ask the manager's permission to park there, the store was packed with Indians doing their Christmas shopping and swiping and swapping and drinking. One huge drunken Indian lunged toward me. I ducked him and he went crashing over a counter. I stumbled over some dirty little brats being sick and doing everything else on the floor while stuffing their pockets with anything and everything they could grab off the counters or out of boxes under counters. There were a lot of clerks but the place was so jammed and such a bedlam they couldn't possibly keep an eye on them all. I had to push my way through all this to reach the manager's office in the rear where I found him buried in heaps of pelts being brought in by the Indian trappers to trade. He finally looked up from his check writing long enough to say, "Sure," to my question.

I thought often that evening of what my mother used to tell me about the Indians among whom she was born and raised in northern Wisconsin. She said an Indian and firewater did not mix well, and the Indians themselves knew it, so when liquor found its way up into that country they would arrange to have half the tribe go on a spree one time and the other half the next time. The sober half would hide all the weapons and keep those celebrating from hurting each other or getting into trouble.

One time too many of them got drunk and descended upon my grandfather's cabin with evil intent. They succeeded in breaking down the door. Grandfather had been sharpening his axes and they were fortunately inside the cabin. So he stood in the doorway with the biggest sharpest one raised over his head. Afraid they would charge in under the axe, my grandmother got her large kettle of hot water into a furious boil on the stove behind him and stood there threatening to scald the first head that dared too close. They were obviously more afraid of the hot water than the axe. They held a consultation and finally departed after going into the barn and turning the cattle loose and cutting all the grain sacks open. The sober ones who had tried hard to manage the situation came around next day to apologize and explain that they had to let them do some mischief before they could get them away.

I had met several of the Indians around Sturgeon Lake when fishing there with Jack. They were all so very friendly with him and seemed a good thrifty bunch living in some well built comfortable homes. The children had the advantage of a very fine big school there.

Then, after sixteen hours of sleep, I felt pretty good but a bit weak and fooled around all day taking pictures and changing a flat tire. A sudden warm wind swooped down, one of those chinooks, and raised thermometers to 34 above.

32.   SOUTH TO EDMONTON

The following day it was cold again and the clock heater in the jeep quit functioning. When I finally got the motor started the gears would hardly shift and the clutch was not working properly, but I was able to drive to a garage in High Prairie where they found nothing wrong except that the clutch had loosened a little.

Freezing and thawing makes worse road conditions than continuous freezing and I found a sudden, funny, short but terribly steep hump twelve miles from Canyon Creek. It was covered with glare ice. Half way up my wheels started spinning, and then I started sliding back down. That was a horrible feeling— the only time in all my driving that the outfit was out of control. It was NO FUN but in those few seconds I thanked my lucky stars I wasn't on one of those mountainsides up the highway where I would have dropped down into oblivion if I slid off the road. As long as I was going back anyway I thought it better to try to drive back than to just let her keep on sliding. I went into reverse and gave her the gas. But it was getting dark and things were happening so fast it was hard to keep track of where the rear end of the blamed trailer was going. Even though there wasn't a very deep ditch, if the trailer had gone an inch further off the right hand side of the road, it would have been a job for a big tractor to get me up and going again. In fact it might have been enough of a tilt to tip me over — and think what a mess there would have been to clean up inside.

I sat there for a while watching cars try to make that little hill and spin and skid and try and try again . It was not a safe place to be sitting. The first truck which came by was hauling a big load of lumber. The nice young driver insisted that with his heavy load to hold him down he'd have good enough traction to pull me up. His wheels spun even before he got hooked on to me. I was worried for a minute when that huge load of lumber started sliding back toward me.

I began desperately throwing a lot of Alaska gravel under his wheels. I had a big bag full on the front bumper. That gravel wasn't enough to get us started pulling up the hill. He took my shovel and probed into the banks on the other side of the road until he found some good sand. Then, by sanding a good stretch of the hill we finally reached the top. I handed him two dollars. But he wouldn't take more than one. He said, "I don't want to take any of your money. You have to work for a living too and it ain't no easy job traveling round taking pictures like you do."

I was almost sorry I had offered him anything. It was the very first time on the whole trip I had offered any money to any of the countless people who had helped me. I knew positively that they would have been either insulted or hurt. Their genuine friendliness and eagerness to be kind and helpful was so wonderful and so completely obvious.

I explained to this chap that I'd like so much to treat him to a good dinner but since there didn't seem to be any place to pull off to park there so that I could cook it I was hoping he would buy himself some beer or a lunch as a treat on me when he got to a lunch room. He said he'd do that since it was getting so late he wouldn't get home in time for supper, but that the one dollar would be enough.

I'm sorry to note the comparison, but could one expect to help so generously offered in the states?

When Mrs. King wrote me of her car trouble, she said she was towed fifty miles into Whitehorse — for a piece of pie.

When I pulled into Canyon Creek on Lesser Slave Lake to park that night, I remembered only too well what happened when I stopped over there on my way up and hooked up to the wrong current. The accident of burning out the frig motor wasn't such a tragedy BUT the unnecessary wait for new one caused me the most serious loss of time of the whole trip. Those twenty or more days would have taken me into the Matanuska Valley in Alaska at their harvest time and on through Anchorage and back to the highway via the Tok Cut-off. What I couldn't do to that Marvel Company for not complying with my request as per my telegram!

It taught me a very costly lesson. When dealing with some company with whom you are not acquainted, spend the money to telephone, talk to the boss, and get his promise to see to it that you order is attended to immediately.

This time in Canyon Creek I used my Kohler.

Going through Smith the next day I caused a panic at sight of my outfit. The folks were afraid I was going to hit every car that was there, smash the pumps and crash into the gas station. When the man came out I said, "Maybe I'd better not get has here for fear that woman will have hysterics again."

I didn't finish the sentence before he was rushing back through the station yelling, "Mama! Mama! Come out here!"

Out came the little woman to the jeep reaching out both hands to shake hands with me, almost in tears of joy, begging for forgiveness for acting so badly.

"I was so nervous that day," she said, "after those two school teachers bumped into my husband's car, and him in it — and I never did have no confidence in women drivers — that is, not until now that I know you. They told me after you was here that time that you was going way to Alaska, and all alone, and driving that thing, and oh I been hoping and praying that you'd get there and back safe. I never knew any woman that had that much courage. I been telling pa I hoped you'd stop by here so's we'd see you if you ever got back. Pa said I acted so bad he didn't think you'd ever stop by here again. And now, God bless you, you did."

I sure did hate to cut Athabasca out of my return trip, but here at Smith there was a new short cut just opened which made the distance to Edmonton 40 or 50 miles shorter, and everyone said the other road through Athabasca was rougher than ever.

The new road was gravel but good and wide. There was so much ice and snow I had to keep chains on all day. It was a lonely road with not a single sign of habitation for 40 miles. I found a gas station near Flatbush where I pulled in for the night. In order not to block the drive I had to pull in so far that I had a devil of a time backing out of the drifts in the morning.

I made the hundred miles to Edmonton in four hours. When I hit pavement 20 miles north of Edmonton it was a divine feeling as I had completely forgotten what it was like.

33.   BACK TO THE MIDWEST

The next morning Jack turned up with a nice invitation to New Year's dinner with his married children who lived in Edmonton.

After a day of shopping and seeing the city, when I was ready to hook up and pull out, Jack noticed that the weight of the trailer on the jeep was pulling the frame away from the body. The frame had a bend in it which looked bad. So I hauled through town to the south and where there was another very nice trailer park, unhooked again and took the jeep to a nearby welding shop to be fixed.

Before I got up next morning there was a pounding at my door—a newspaper reporter. The next day's paper came out with a big picture of the trailer and jeep across the top center of the front page with a three-column of story under headlines, "Girl Photographer Tours North Dragging Her Home Behind Her." Under the picture it said, "Home Sweet Home to Woman Author."

The trailer was described in every detail, of course, this time calling it a "dream boat" and there was even a paragraph leading one to think I'm not very pleasant to early morning callers. Under "Roused Sleeper" it said, "Along the smooth sidewall of the trailer house a door knob fitted neatly into the surface. A sleepy voice uttered an 'Ugh' to the vigorous 9:00 a.m. pounding. Then 'Wait till I dress. I'll only be half an hour.' The time finally got down to five minutes. Then a tousled head appeared in the doorway and a tall, striking figure in maroon housecoat appeared below it."

Then, right in the beginning of the article, the author called me, "youthful," so I've more than forgiven her for waking me.

That morning in Red Deer the thermometer jumped suddenly to 50 degrees above zero—another chinook. The same day, Los Angeles was registering 29 degrees above.

It was very windy and difficult driving that day with a bad dust storm north of Calgary. Before I reached High River the wind became terrific and some people warned me that cars were being blown off the road. I wanted to reach High River to park in a spot I knew, and I felt fairly confident and that my eight tons of weight would help hold me on the ground. And I thought the wind would die down after dark, but it didn't.

People in High River were having a time anchoring everything down which had not already been blown away. Two trailers were parked there and one was blown over on its side against the other.

I parked back of a service station in a partially sheltered spot and let down the stabilizing jacks under the four corners of the trailer. They were all bent next morning. The wind kept up all night and it is a wonder I didn't get tipped over.

It not only was still blowing in the morning but also snowing. There was about a foot of the light fluffy stuff on the ground being whipped around so it was almost impossible to see the road. I even went right through the town of Stavely without seeing anything. I had wanted to stop there to gas up and say hello to a garage man who had been very nice to me with my tire troubles on my way up.

When I was ready to pull out of Lethbridge the next morning it was 27 below at 10:00 a.m. and the jeep refused to start. I fussed and fussed with hot water, hot oil, electric radiators, etc. but had to get a wrecker to pull me to get started. Then I headed for the good garage I knew down at the corner in Coutts where I was determined I'd get a decent heater put into my jeep water system. The man there at Horner's Garage remembered me and he installed a heater element in the hose between the radiator and block and that ended my cold weather starting troubles.

No trouble going through customs.

Back on old Route 2 once more I rolled along at about 50 miles an hour into Havre. When Norm Odden came back to his office to do some work that evening he found me parked in my old place back of his shop.

If my trailer had not been so good and tight it would have been impossible to keep it warm enough while traveling to avoid the freezing of water pipes. The Kohler running in the jeep kept me nice and warm and the electric steam radiator seemed enough to keep the chill out of the trailer. The only water pipes I had to watch were the ones going to the shower bath. They ran along over the wheel housing where there was evidently not enough insulation.

Going through the town of Minot, North Dakota was difficult. It seems so hard for the towns to get their streets cleared of snow during any of the bad storms and the deep icy ruts which form and last for weeks made driving hazardous.

Following truck routes and finding gas stations and parking places was always my best bet when traveling conditions were bad. Near the town of Sawyer I spent the night among dozens of coal trucks. A whole fleet of them were held over there because the road into the mine was still blocked.

Then it began to snow and blow again and I bucked the wind at about 20 miles an hour all day to Carrington where I again found the only clear and open space to park near the grain elevators.

Next day it blew harder than ever but the wind was with me so I sailed along all morning until I turned east. Then it was hard going again into Moorehead. There I visited the Pierce Trailer Sales and again and they sent me out to their new trailer park for the night. They had 80 trailers parked there.

From then on I picked the most level roads, stopping in Alexandria and Olivia in Minnesota.

At a truck checking point in the eastern Iowa I drove onto the scales just for fun to see whether I still weighed eight tons. Sure enough — a little over 16,600 pounds. No matter how many of my supplies I used up I seemed to replenish them with something equally as heavy.

The jeep wasn't running well. I guess most folks wondered that it ran at all. It finally got so bad that I limped into a garage in Maysville, northwest of Davenport, Iowa and found a valve busted. A nice bright chap who was a hustler went right to work on it. That garage was a family affair with two or three brothers and dad working as mechanics, sister Pat keeping the books, and Ma Ferris seeing to it that they all ate, practically stuffing food into them while they worked when they were too busy to stop for meals.

When I crossed the Mississippi at Davenport, the toll man stuck his head in the jeep and asked, "Where's the Eskimo?" and then, "Didn't you bring back a bear?" I guess I should have brought back Peater.

It was a jungle from one route to another through Illinois to try to avoid icy hills. Left 6 at Geneseo, up to 18 to 92, a very good road. Everything seemed to be going fine and I was zipping along when — snap! Rear right axle broke!

So now I had use for the spare I had carried all the way to Alaska and back. It was the shorter one of the two rear axles. When the jeep dealer at home had filled the list of spare parts which were then required in order to obtain the permit to travel the Alaska Highway, he did not have the longer axle which I wanted.

I thought if I broke any it would probably be the longer one in the rear and sure enough that was the one I did break up in Fort St. John. I had tried several times to trade this shorter one but now I was sure glad that I had been unsuccessful of getting rid of it. A garage man came out from Serena, a couple of miles ahead, and he had the proper tools to fix it for me promptly.

The terribly icy roads seemed to end abruptly at the Illinois - Indiana border and I was so familiar with that last lap of road that I kept on going until, late the night of February 6th, I pulled up alongside the Liberty Coach Company factory in Bremen. The warm welcome by the Lemans at the hotel made me forget how tired I was. And they had a bushel of mail for me.

Next day a migraine.

34. A BRIGHT IDEA

The men at the factory were all so amazed to see how the trailer looked. You could hardly tell the difference between it and the new ones rolling off the assembly line, that is, until you examined it and saw all the reinforcing I had done to the underneath frame, tongue, etc. Spencer had written me that they would put a new frame under it but it was soon evident that no new frame they were making around there would be anywhere near as strong as the one I now had. The man from the frame shop said, "We couldn't possibly use all that metal in our frames — it would increase the cost of the trailers too much."

Then we held many conferences about a heavier carriage with bigger wheels and tires and MUCH BETTER BRAKES, but I got nowhere with any of those things which to me seemed so very important.

They were, however, interested in seeing how the trailer had stood the cold and said they were insulating their new trailers better. So they tore off all the outside of my trailer and found the insulation wet from the accumulation of frost, especially around the bottom. They put in fresh insulation and more of it, and then a layer of aluminum foil inside the masonite walls.

They rebuilt the bedroom into a much more practical and attractive arrangement with the bed placed lengthwise. A nice vanity dresser replaced the atrocious storage space from which things could not be retrieved.

The interior finish of the trailer had remained just exactly like new, but that pain in the neck which had been called an oil heater — it had given up the ghost completely when I rolled into the factory grounds and was immediately tossed into the junk heap. Then they began experimenting with a new heater, tore up the floor and put in new ducts to carry the heat front and aft, and insisted that it would do the job in Alaska or anywhere.

While all this was begin done, Mr. Spencer asked me whether I did not think it would be worthwhile to fly back up to Alaska to talk to the military personnel about using trailers to ease the critical housing shortage. I told him the big problem would be getting them up there.

The fact that I, a woman traveling alone, had succeeded in hauling a big heavy trailer all the way up there AND back was giving the trailer manufacturers and the people in Alaska the idea that, after all, it COULD be done. And this big Liberty trailer would probably make the warmest, most comfortable living quarters of any trailer made if it could be successfully and economically transported to that far north country.

Spencer was willing to gamble my airfare and expenses and I was willing to gamble my time and energy to fly back up and try to promote some deals.

Leaving Chicago at midnight and reaching Fairbanks at four in the afternoon March 1, 1949 was certainly the other extreme of traveling.

Back to Lehman's Hotel in Breman, Indiana where the Liberty trailer was made.

35.   A RETURN TO THE NORTH

After landing at Ladd Field in Fairbanks, I looked over a military trailer park project with the officer in charge. He informed me that General Gaffney wouldn't be back until the end of the week. Since Gaffney was in charge of the base and the only high officer in Alaska all interested in trailers, I had to wait to see him. Meanwhile, I interviewed the bank presidents about financing some trailer purchases, talked with the mayor, the city manager, the travel service, the Chamber of Commerce and anyone and everyone who could possibly be interested in or have anything to do with the housing problem.

The housing problem was affecting me first hand now that I found myself up there without my living quarters along with me. I was lucky enough to get into the second best hotel in town — a pretty wild place marked "Off Limits" for military. I slid the dresser in front of the door and wasn't disturbed except by repeated gentle knocks on the door by a male acquaintance from further down the highway who was in town for the carnival. He would depart without trying to force his way in, but kept living in hopes.

Some of the officers at Ladd Field arranged for me to ride the hundred miles down to Big Delta in the mail truck. Another disadvantage in being up there without my outfit was no jeep to run around in. The mail truck had to pass through Eielson Field and at both gates they put up a big fuss about my being in the mail truck; it was against the rules. The driver regretted not having locked me in back with the mail bags.

I had heard that Colonel Shelor, in charge of Big Delta, would never listen to mention of the word trailer. When I met him next morning I asked him why. He said emphatically, "I'm NOT going to have any of my personnel going outdoors to the latrine in Alaska weather."

"I wish you might have seen the trailer I brought up here," I said. Then I explained that all the good new trailers were complete with their own private baths and all modern conveniences.

"What's that you say?" So his opinion of trailers changed immediately and after a good long talk with him on ideas for a trailer park and other details he told me he thought trailers might be a practical method for easing the serious housing shortage and said he hoped I could convince his superior officer, General Scott, over at Anchorage. Then he said he would help me in making an appointment to meet General Scott who was at this moment on his way up the highway, driving over the road to investigate its condition.

Finding a place to sleep at the Delta was harder than I anticipated. I thought the Triangle Lodge had rooms. They didn't, but Jean Riley said she could rent me a cot in the pantry off the kitchen. So there I slept as well as I could among the potatoes, olives and canned peaches.

While waiting for the bus to go back to Fairbanks the next morning, a young chap with a camera slung round his neck, the fuzzy-wuzzy start of a beard and a yellow jeep came along and asked me whether I'd care to ride up with him. James Rose, his name.

Was he full of questions and enthusiasm! He seemed the right type for Alaska all right. He and his wife, baby, his best buddy and his wife had decided they wanted to live in Alaska. He was making this quick trip by himself to look the place over and try to pick suitable homestead sites.

I gave him all the advice and suggestions I could think of and by the time we got up the highway near where the Canadays live I decided that nothing could help him more than to become acquainted with that fine, intelligent family who had made such a good go of homesteading. The Canadays started from nothing and worked up to a good livelihood for themselves.

When I interviewed General Gaffney he gave me some shocking reports on the housing situation and quoted some figures which took my breath away. It had cost the military $67,000 per family unit for regular military housing there at Ladd Filed, and they had tried a Lustron Prefab steel house which cost them $42,000 to set up ready for occupancy.

Gaffney was building a trailer park where there were already a few trailers parked. He said they could use 40 to 60 more and had suggested that the government should purchase trailers to rent to the service men. But some of the powers-that-be said they weren't going to have the army go into the real estate business.

No one up there had been willing to offer any help in the way of financing the purchase of trailers by individuals, especially by service men stationed in that country for only two years. I talked with Cap Lathrop and he finally said he would consider doing it for some with good character references.

For the latter part of my stay in Fairbanks I was fortunate in being able to move into the Nordale and occupy Mary Anderson's room while Mary spent a few days in Anchorage.

Before I left for Anchorage, Cap Lathrop asked me where I was going to stay. I told him I had wired for a room at a small hotel where I was told there might be chance of getting in. "Oh, you must stay at our hotel," he said, and dictated a letter to his secretary for me to take to the Westward Hotel manager, and was I glad to have that letter! Out of politeness I called at the hotel where I had wired to cancel my reservation. It wasn't necessary. They had no room.

The Westward was a magnificent hotel and the corner room on the top floor to which I was led made me think I was in one of the most expensive rooms in the Statler in Washington. I heaved a sigh of relief the next morning when the desk clerk informed me that I was paying only $6.50. That was the same price I had paid for the dingy room in the joint in Fairbanks.

Hotel service in a tent" meant four cot beds, one in each corner of a bare square tent. Summer tourists paid $10 a night to sleep on one of these cots.

The flight to Anchorage was over such cold, desolate looking, snow-covered, mountainous country, it made me wonder whether Alaska was worth the $7,200,000 we paid Russia for it.

Fort Richardson, which includes Elmendorf Field, covers about 200 square miles. I interviewed General Scott and colonels galore in a big building they called the Kremlin. Many of them, hitherto opposed to trailers, like Colonel Shelor were intrigued by the idea of having the deluxe models with private baths.

Whether they ever realized it or appreciated it, I certainly did a lot for the trailer industry on that flying trip through Alaska.

The trip down to Juneau was a terribly rough one. I thought I was a good sailor and a good flyer, but the terrific wind storm buffeted that two-motored plane around so much I nearly gave up the ghost. A little

four-year-old orphan Eskimo boy sitting across the aisle from me stood the trip much better than I. He was being sent to school down near Juneau, a charming little fellow with perfect manners and evidently thoroughly accustomed to air travel.

In Juneau all the better hotels were full, but I finally found a room — a room with two of its windows blown out — that's how hard the wind had been blowing that day.

It seems so silly to have Juneau the capital of Alaska. It can be reached only by air or water and is so far removed from all of Alaska that I am certainly in sympathy with the idea now being promoted by many to move the capital to Palmer, near Anchorage.

If the government offices are moved away from Juneau there won't be much left of the town, now that the big old gold mine has been closed, probably never to open operations again. There are just a few square feet of level ground in the town. Each little narrow street runs along no more than a block or two before it bumps up against a perpendicular mountainside — every street except one which runs down to the little harbor. Though there are bars and the swank Baranoff Hotel, the government employees would have a lot more fun up in Anchorage with its Main Street boasting 66 or more liquor dispensaries.

I called on Governor Gruening and then spent considerable time in the office of the Alaska Housing Authority. I met Ken Kadow, who directs the Alaska Field Staff of the Department of the Interior. Mr. Kadow has been struggling for some time to get trailers to Alaska to help the housing situation, but there were the inevitable stumbling blocks of getting them up there and financing them.

There being no one else left to see I boarded a plane the 17th of March for Seattle and Chicago, glad to be on the big four-motored stratocruisers again, just in case we should meet stormy weather like that between Anchorage and Juneau. But those long plane rides are as tiresome as long bus rides. I hope soon, for those cross-country flights they will have planes with berths as they have on the trans-ocean airliners. I simply can't sleep sitting up as some people do.

36. THIRD TIME TO BREMEN

Then back to Bremen. They had told me they would take my trailer right into the shop when I left and do the work on it. I moved all my things out of it and expected to find it finished. They not only hadn't started the work but had let it stand outside and with no heat in it, of course, the water pump had frozen and broken. I could have drained it before I left, but oh no, they were going to move it right into the warm shop.

I began to try again for more efficient brakes. They called in a representative from the Warner Brake Company. He took me to lunch. He admitted that the brakes used on trailers were not adequate. "But the trailer industry has no ethics," he said.

I went over to Chicago and spent a few days at the big International Trailer Show looking over about sixty different makes of trailers. I hunted up several of the manufacturers of frames and parts and materials used in making trailers. Some of them were frank enough to give me their opinions of various makes of trailers. But the public was looking at the trailers generally with an eye only for attractive appearance and the charm and convenience of interior design.

Spencer stole the show, as he always does, this time with a double decker. The upper floor with its three bedrooms slide down over the roof of the first floor for travel and then, when and if the hydraulic hoist worked it could be raised to make a two story house. As for roadability — Lord forbid anyone trying to travel with it. They had a devil of a time getting anyone to risk his life hauling it from Bremen to Chicago. It sold for $7,000 to $8,000 and several orders were turned in. There are evidently people who can see advantages I cannot see in having a house on wheels remaining in one spot—a house at that price with its limitations in size and design and its remoteness from anything which could possibly be considered attractive by those with any taste for architectural style or charm or beauty.

Finally, when ready to pull out from Bremen, the Warner brake man told me to drive around by way of Elkhart where he would have my brakes pulled apart and examined. They found the parts were not a proper fit so they had the drums honed out, gave me some new linings and put them in much better working order.

While waiting around for the brake job I visited several trailer factories in that vicinity. Again I wondered how long it will be before a really conscientious effort goes into the manufacture of trailer coaches planned and designed by intelligent engineers. I guess not until the housing shortage eases up and fewer people are obliged to use them as living quarters even when permanently located.

I drove round to the Willys-Overland factory in Toledo. Having given them so very much publicity I thought they might show some appreciation. Their public relations department took me out to an elegant lunch, had me tell them a lot about my trip, got what they considered a very good story. What did I get out of it besides lunch? exactly zero. Jeeps are made to haul one-and-a-half tons, not eight tons.

When I went on a tour through that plant it seemed to me the busiest man in the factory was the one whose job it was to go around and erase from the walls the dirty things the workmen kept scrawling in big bold letters about the management. And when I saw how the jeeps were stamped out and thrown together I wondered how any of them ran.

That factory was such a contrast to the Kohler plant up near Sheboygan in Wisconsin. It was very obvious there that all the employees held great loyalty and admiration for the management. Every workman there seemed to be proud to be doing his very best and the management showed its appreciation in many ways. The workmen there never feared being laid off. If there were ever any slack times they all stayed on the job but worked shorter hours. There were men who had been with that company for fifty years and a large club of members who had been there more than twenty five years.

They were very interested to see how my light plant had stood the trip. I sent it in to them and they returned it to me looking like a brand new one. It had really stood the abuses of such travel famously, jolting over all those thousands of miles of rough road, running on any and every kind of fuel I could find, and never failing to start no matter how far below zero the thermometer fell. It was by far the best and most reliable piece of equipment I had with me and contributed to my comfort and convenience more than anything else.

In an effort to find a trailer manufacturing company which looked really good I ran up to visit the Vagabond Coach Company at New Hudson, Michigan. I didn't spend much time there, but what I saw pleased me very much. It seemed to me that without expanding too fast or trying to make unreasonable profits or operating in elaborate style, they had an exceptionally fine outfit with the same sort of good spirit existing between labor and management which I found at Kohler. I consider their trailer a better engineered product than any I saw rolling off any other assembly line. I certainly admire them for thinking that a trailer is MADE FOR TRAVEL and should therefore be made on the good sound principles of engineering which considers road worthyness, strength, lightness, ease of hauling, durability, etc.

They feel that 33 feet is too long for those going to be hauled by passenger cars, and they make 29 feet their limit. In that 29 feet they put very practical and attractive designs of living quarters with a complete bath. It is an all welded steel tube body frame and the exterior is completely covered with aluminum. It has ample insulation of the finest quality and expertly applied with careful workmanship throughout. Most important to me is the very strong frameunderneath. I haven't seen any as good as the Vagabond truss type frame and it is now covered with an under-sheathing of heavy steel which tightly seals it — an extremely valuable feature.

The atmosphere seemed CLEAN about that Vagabond factory and it was a real pleasure to nose around for a few days.

37. HOME SWEET HOME

I like the road through Ontario better than the one through the crowded cities along the lake in the states. I went through customs at Sarnia slick as a whistle — old license plates and all. It hadn't dawned on me till March 30th that I'd be needing new plates April 1st. I wired for them to be sent to me in care of Bemis Motors in Brattleboro, not knowing where I'd be or when, and thinking that if it came to the worst and I was arrested or stopped some place and prevented from proceeding further I could phone or wire Mr. Bemis to forward them to me.

Over the Lewiston Bridge into the states again. The customs officers were all so intrigued with my outfit and where I'd been with it they never gave license plates a thought and all of them, at least six, had to see the inside of the trailer and ask questions about Alaska and the highway.

On through New York state I thought surely my old bright green license plates would be noticed, but they weren't. When I thought everything was going nicely, there was a bang. Another broken axle! I had to unhook and drive the jeep on its front drive six miles into Geneva. A big garage there had an axle and all necessary tools but it made me so sick to watch the way the boys insisted upon hammering the old one out I could hardly stand it. Instead of using the axle pulling device they used a sledge hammer with such ruthless blows I thought they'd ruin the gears completely. They damaged them, but there seemed nothing I could do about it. It was Saturday morning and the boys were afraid they might have to work a little longer that afternoon. This was the states again, not Canada.

In trying to avoid the hills around Utica I tried some different roads, all of which seemed to get me into steeper and steeper country. I never did notice all those steep hills when scooting around with a car but now my eight tons made them seem ten times as steep.

Nearing home and being so familiar with the way through Troy I kept driving long after dark that night. Then the next day took me over the old Molly Stark Trail. It would have been mighty embarrassing if I needed help on the hills between Bennington and Brattleboro, and I almost did. My eagerness to get home made me take some of the downgrades a little too fast and the strain I put on the trailer brakes was so hard on them that by the time I reached Brattleboro I had none left.

The jeep brakes were also practically gone, so instead of giving my old hometown a good show by pulling down through Main Street I didn't dare take a chance on High Street Hill and crawled around the back way.

At the Bemis garage the boys came rushing out with my new license plates and I never could understand why they were in such a desperate hurry to get them on for me. I'd been running on the old ones eleven days after they expired.

Notes on Photos

Page	Collection Number
Front cover	B.89.4.365
	B.89.4.6
7	B.89.420
22	B.89.4.4
26	B.89.4.9
31	B.89.4.91
35	B.89.4.145
43	B.89.4.35
48	B.89.4.37
49	B.89.4.51
57	B.89.4.164
61	B.62.x.15.3 (US Army)
	B.89.4.212 (US Army)
62	B.89.4.213 (US Army)
	B.89.4.217 (US Army)
63	B.89.4.211 (US Army)
	B.89.4.215 (US Army)
64	B.62.x.15.18 (US Army)
	B.62.x.15.15 (US Army)
67	B.89.4.175
70	B.89.4.243
74	B.89.4.290
79	B.89.4.320
83	B.89.4.343
88	B.89.4.274
97	B.89.4.416
102	B.89.4.492
105	B.89.4.383
116	B.89.4.427
117	B.89.4.348
119	B.89.4.166
	B.89.4.172
121	B.89.4.441
128	B.89.4.449
131	B.89.4.450
149	B.89.4.488
152	B.89.4.413
160	B.89.4.210
Back cover	B.89.4.450

Dawson Creek, British Columbia, Mile 0 Alaska Highway, 1948